NUNC COGNOSCO EX PARTE

THOMAS J. BATA LIBRARY
TRENT UNIVERSITY

THE LONDON ADVENTURE

By the Same Author

The Terror
The Bowmen
Dr. Stiggins
The Great Return
Hieroglyphics
The House of Souls—*Including* The Great
God Pan and The Three Impostors
The Hill of Dreams
The Chronicle of Clemendy
War and the Christian Faith
The Secret Glory
Far Off Things
Things Near and Far
The Shining Pyramid

THE LONDON ADVENTURE
OR THE ART OF WANDERING
BY ARTHUR MACHEN

SECOND IMPRESSION

LONDON: MARTIN SECKER

First Published   August, 1924
Reprinted   October, 1924

LONDON : MARTIN SECKER (LTD.) 1924

I

THERE is a certain tavern in the north-western parts of London which is so remote from the tracks of men and so securely hidden that few people have ever suspected its existence. For, in the first place, it is quite off the high roads of the leafy quarter once familiarly known as "the Wood," and then again, the byway in which it is situated does not suggest the presence of any house of public entertainment. Here are modest residences of stucco and grey brick, built for quiet people in the late 'thirties and early 'forties; their front gardens planted with trees of all sorts and varieties before the period when somebody settled that the only tree for London was the plane. Here and there in these gardens there survives an old gnarled thorn, a remnant, I suspect, of the time when "the Wood" was really a wood or a waste. There are no shops in the street, passengers are rare, and the whole region breathes quiet and repose. But far, as I say, from the high road, one of the modest residences displays a sign before its door, and is, in fact, a tavern. It lacks not custom. Jobbing gardeners drink gravely on one side of the establishment, and play games of Dominoes and Darts with the utmost decency; on the other there are some quiet bookmakers, sculptors, poets, and men of letters.

In this pleasant and retired spot I was sitting not long ago, enjoying gin and that great luxury and blessing of idleness, concerning which so much cant and false doctrine have been preached. It is, no doubt, perfectly true that a few men, a very few men, are born into the world to whom a great task has been assigned by the Almighty, and they are to perform this task or fail at their peril. Woe to the prophet who will not prophesy: doubtless. It would have been woe to Turner the painter if, instead of painting, he had devoted all his energies to that queer, disreputable life he led on the riverside by Chelsea, where he was thought to be an odd specimen of the retired mariner. There are the prophets in words and in paint and in other forms who have their work to do and must do it. But, for the rest of us, our " work " is but the curse of Adam, the slavery that we have to endure; about as blessed as

THE LONDON ADVENTURE

oakum-picking and limestone quarrying and treadmill climbing and the other employments of the poor fellows that we call convicts, as if we were not as much convicts as they. We have been convicted of the offence of being born, and the sentence of the Court has been that we shall earn an honest living : an awful and a dreadful doom, if we had the courage to confess it. For, if we see clearly, we shall see that the men we call convicts and criminals have evidently chosen the better part. They have refused to abide the dreadful sentence that was pronounced against them at the moment of their birth. They have revolted, in one way or another, and the plan of things has got hold of them and pronounced a second sentence against them, and enslaved them, as it believes, in a much worse fashion. But the scheme of things is mistaken. It is not a much worse fashion. The convicted criminal is the victim of greater force. He cannot help himself : true : but he has no responsibility for himself or for his actions. He may think oakum-picking a loathsome occupation for a man ; still, he is forced to do it, the choice is not his, but that of others. Violent bodily compultion absolves him from all sense of degradation : if there be anything of the kind it is on the shoulders of those who order his occupations and compel him to follow them.

But this consolation is withheld from those whom cowardice or lack of enterprise or incapacity keeps in the narrow way of what is called honesty. It is, no doubt, sad enough, if you earn your ounces of bread and ounces of meat and ounces of potatoes by compliance with the strict demands of the warders and the Governor of the gaol, but it is surely much worse when the said ounces—that is livelihood—are purchased by shameful insincerities and smooth compliance. There are men—many of them—whose life it is to be shamed and insulted on Monday and then to be the good companions of the oppressor on Tuesday—lest they lose their living on Wednesday. There was once a very eminent journalist of Carmelite House. He was not only the distinguished servant but the friend of the late Lord Northcliffe, and he thought, no doubt, that he could make a personal and confidential appeal to the beloved " chief." And so John Robinson wrote to the effect that times were hard, that the income-tax on a bachelor was heavy—and could his old friend increase his salary by a little ?

He had his reply. It was posted up on the wall

of some Common Room of the *Daily Mail*, for everybody, down to the office boy, to see. It ran somewhat to this effect.

" John Robinson asks me to increase his salary. He says that, as a bachelor, he is very heavily taxed. I would point out to John that he can easily remedy this part of his troubles by marrying one of my pretty typists on *The Times*."

I never heard that John Robinson beat the wretch who perpetrated this infamy. I think he remained in the service of Carmelite House. Probably, John shrugged his shoulders and said to himself, " A man has got to get a living." But he could have picked pockets, he could have become a burglar, a confidence trickster, a three-card man on a race train. There were many courses open to John ; and if he had been caught and convicted he could have got a living in gaol by picking oakum—and held up his head. In gaol you have to obey the rules and the warders : hard rules and hard men. Still, that is the game that has to be played in gaol ; there is no shame in it.

Hence, I say, my profound contempt for all those who praise " work " and the ways of honest living, which are, mostly, degradations somewhat below those experienced by the procurer of Soho. Hence, my profound gratitude for the bliss of idleness, for the happy state in which you survey the universe, somewhat in the manner of Socrates, who, so far as I remember, never did an honest day's work in his life, and made a very fine end. And, in this spirit, I was relishing the savours of things in general, thanking Heaven that I was at last, after long years, an idler once more, and sipping my gin and water, when a man entered the retired tavern which I have endeavoured to describe. He sat down opposite to me. His manner was threatening. He said in a very meaning tone :

"The leaves are beginning to come out"—and looked hard at me as he said it.

I shuddered. I was very much in the condition of the Young Man in Spectacles—some of my readers may know whom I mean—when he was suddenly accosted in the public-house by the emissary of Lipsius.

"*At the first touch of the hand on his arm the unfortunate man had wheeled round as if spun on a pivot and shrank back with a low, piteous cry, as if some beast were caught in the toils. The blood fled away from the wretch's face, etc. etc.*"

THE LONDON ADVENTURE

So I. I knew what that man meant. I had told him some months before that I was to write a book about London, that it was to be a really great book, this time. But, I explained, I was not going to begin writing it till the leaves were out on the trees, since the green leafage of the boughs made such a marvellous contrast with the grim greyness of the streets ; of the streets of which I meant to write : unknown, unvisited squares in Islington, dreary byways in Holloway, places traversed by railway arches and viaducts in the regions of Camden Town.

And well I remember adding how once I had some mission to execute in waste portions of the world down beyond the Surrey Docks. I took an omnibus at the other end of London Bridge and went, I think, by way of Tooley Street, into something unshapen that I had never visited before ; into places that might have been the behind the scenes of the universe ; bearing, indeed, much the same relation to the ordinary London view as do the back of the backcloth and the backs of the wings to the gay set that the audience admires from the stalls. Everything was shapeless, unmeaning, dreary, dismal beyond words ; it was as if one were journeying past the back wall of the everlasting backyard. Then a street of grey brick with stucco mouldings, not much gayer than the blank walls ; and lo ! from the area of one of the sad houses there arose a great glossy billow of the most vivid green surging up from the area pavement half-way the height of the ground floor windows ; a veritable verdant mountain, as blessed as any wells and palm trees in the midst of an African desert. It was a fig tree that had somehow contrived to flourish in this arid waste ; but to me a miracle and a delight as well as a fig tree.

Well ; this was to be the kind of adventure out of which I had agreed to make a book ; and thus it was that I had talked of waiting till the time of the opening of the leaves before I began it ; and thus I shuddered when my friend came into the retired tavern and reminded me that the trees were indeed putting on their green and that so it was time for me to set about my task. Always, or almost always, I have had the horror of beginning a new book. I have burnt my fingers to the bone again and again in the last forty years and I dread the fire of literature. I know what will happen to me, just as the little boy knows what will happen to him when the dear old Head says : " Come to my room after morning school."

However, there was no help for it. The book was to be written; and I bowed my head before the message of the tavern; having, indeed, a very special reverence, almost an unreasoning awe, of signs and intimations given in odd ways in unexpected fashions, in places and surroundings which are generally accounted unreverend enough. In a former book I have described with some minuteness and—may I add—with absolute veracity what strange things I once experienced in chambers in Gray's Inn, in forsaken Rosebery Avenue, in all sorts of down-at-heel and shabby quarters of London; and I have never forgotten my almost incredulous amazement when I found out, seven years afterwards, that some of these experiences of mine had also been experiences of the monks of St. Columba's congregation at Iona in the sixth century—I think it was the sixth—of our era. But so corrupt and bewildered is our nature; on the one hand inclined to the crudest, most bestial materialism, to the simple, easy, natural explanation of all wonders, all miracles; on the other, so sickened with sham marvels, with pantomime-chorus fairies on photographic plates, with ghosts that gibber indeed in the vulgarest, silliest manner possible; so bewildered are we, I say, between these two sides that we hardly dare to testify to the things which we have actually known, seen, experienced with our own senses and our own souls, if these experiences go beyond the limits laid down in some twopenny " science " text-book. The ancients never found America because their " science " told them that when you once passed the Pillars of Hercules the air became full of feathers; and so we fail to discover a better world than America because we cannot find it in our manuals of chemistry, biology, or physiology.

De me fabula ; but I do my best to conquer this " scientific " nonsense; and so, as I have noted, I try to reverence the signs, omens, messages that are delivered in queer ways and queer places, not in the least according to the plans laid down either by the theologians or the men of science. I shall never forget how one such message came to me of a dreadful afternoon some two and a half years ago; to the best of my belief in the January of 1921. I was sitting in a subterranean chamber of a tavern not far removed from that thoroughfare which Sir Philip Gibbs has styled so agreeably—and truthfully, I am sure—the Street of Adventure. It was

THE LONDON ADVENTURE

just beginning to dawn on me after some weeks of doubt and wondering incredulity that I was in the power of certain people who had made up their minds for some unknown reason to subject me to the most shameful and humiliating mortifications that can be conceived.

At all events; here was I on this January afternoon of 1921, sitting at my table in the tavern room, quite overwhelmed with misery and despair. I am a married man, I may say; and so bound by certain just considerations of responsibility. I was not free to throw the money of these people into their collective faces, and then go forth to thieve or forge or rob blind men's dogs, or—in point of fact—to get a small living in a comparatively decent manner. I was to live on and keep those who depended on me by a prostitution of the soul, compared with which the prostitution of the body is a little thing. I was to lick spittle from the office floor. The office boys, the inferior hangers-on and servants of a great newspaper were to know all about it and to jeer at me as I went in and out and passed along the accursed corridors. I was to be pitied by the kindly lad who attended to the telephone, smiled at by the young man who ran the editor's errands.

And the only hopeful end to this purgatory was in itself doom. After I had been tormented sufficiently I should be dismissed : and that meant ruin for my wife and children.

Ah ; if one only had the courage to be truly wise ! True wisdom is in the keeping of the saints—I am not confusing the saints with the bishops who are ready to die on the doorstep of the House of Lords if Marylebone people can get a glass of beer after 10 p.m., or with the ecclesiastics of all grades who have proclaimed their solidarity with the Labour Party. But the wisdom of the saints would have directed me that now the supreme chance of my life had come ; that, here and now, to a wretched Fleet Street reporter, there was offered an opportunity for which many aureoled and glorious ones had sighed in vain. *Ama nesciri et pro nihilo reputari :* so spoke St. Thomas à Kempis, and he was writing to monks, and was probably thinking of the set mortifications of the monastery, of the schemes by which Baronius was wont to be discovered washing dishes when great princes came from afar to the Oratory to see him. But here was the real thing : the true mortifications that burned and scorched to the very marrow, to the inner heart ; the most

THE LONDON ADVENTURE

exquisite joy to the wise, to those that truly know the Gate and the Way. Here was the Shut Palace of the King laid open, here appeared the Bride in the Banqueting House, here from the Engendering of the Crow rose the Son Blest of the Fire. I could almost hear the song of those that feast within :

O pius, O bonus, O placidus sonus, hymnus eorum.

But, alas, I was very far from wise. I sat at my table and ate and drank with a sick heart, with horror and despair very heavy at my heart, that January afternoon. And suddenly a man stood before me and said :

" Ah say, mister, could ya tell me how to spell *exaltavit*. Ma friend and I have been arguing about it, and we thowt ya might be able to tell us : ya seem to be as intelligent looking as anybody here. Ya know the words, ah daresay : *Deposuit potentes de sede, et exaltavit humiles.* Ma friend will have it that there's an ' s ' in ' exaltavit,' but I say ' no.' "

I answered this not very difficult question to the best of my ability, and sat wondering. I think the gentleman stood me a drink in gratitude for the profound scholarship which had confirmed his position, and that we chatted, his friend, himself, and I, for ten minutes or so on indifferent subjects.

THE LONDON ADVENTURE

Then we went on our several ways : I, if I remember rightly, to interview a gentleman of no particular consequence, living at the other end of nowhere, on a matter quite devoid of interest. But I had those words sounding in my ears all the while : *et exaltavit humiles*. I wondered ; and again heard, *et exaltavit humiles*. And then I began to hope a little, to lift up a little corner of the black curtain of despair : *et exaltavit humiles*.

Now, to put an end at once to all false mysteries and mystifications : I may say that I got to know the man who had come up to me in the tavern fairly well. The only real mystery about him was his pronunciation of the Latin words : he said " exaltahvit " not " exaltehvit," and I have often wondered how he came by these true church tones. He was a man from the provinces, as I have indicated, and was following in London, not very successfully, some byway of commercial journalism, trying to get advertisements, we will say, for the "Basket Makers' Gazette." He was, I should think, a very good and kindly fellow. We used to meet, for a year or more, at pretty frequent intervals, in the underground room of the tavern and talk about things over our tankards ; chiefly, if I remember, about a patent

THE LONDON ADVENTURE

penknife that Mr. Harrison wished to put on the market. When I last saw him, he told me that he had got a new job and " stood to be lucky " ; and very glad I was to hear it. He was one of the two or three of the messengers that I have met in my life, and I never think of them without great wonder, awe, and reverence. Not in any personal way : when one hears Mass one does not want to know who or what the priest is, whether he is a good judge of poetry or, unfortunately, ill-tempered and over-fond of garlic. He is clothed in the vestments of his office, his gestures are not his own, he speaks words assigned to him from afar.

I asked Mr. Harrison the second or third time of our meeting as to his interest in a verse of the *Magnificat*. I found that his source was not the Breviary, but some poem of Longfellow's about Robert of Sicily ; and—I am not quite sure—but I think that a possible cinema picture was in the background of these enquiries. But these words : *et exaltavit humiles*, sounded still in my heart—till they came true.

With due reserves and exceptions. For I was not *humilis* ; or I would have taken the way of the true wisdom which I have indicated above ; the way of those who rejoice in the sharpest mortifications, and are only glad when they are utterly despised. I was certainly not *humilis*, but I was certainly *humiliatus*; and the good God is content with a little when He cannot get all. He remembereth " that we are but dust "; and as Father Stanton said, commenting on this text : " You can't expect very much from dust." And as to the *exaltavit* : I think that I still recognise my old friends when I meet them in the street, my exaltation simply consisting in the fact that, so far, I have been permitted to live in a very modest way without swallowing an insult with every crust and excrement with every cup : and that is enough of exaltation for me, and bliss indeed, such as I never hoped to gain on that dreary January afternoon of 1921, when the plain man asked me how I would spell *exaltavit*.

It was just a coincidence ? It may be so ; and I am too keenly aware of the dangers and follies of credulity to deny that it may have been so. Yet, I am a practical man above all things, and coincidence or no coincidence, I know that I was comforted and sustained and enabled by that word through many months of horrible and shameful suffering. And, -on the whole, I am really inclined to believe that this is the way in which things are done ; that the betting man who backs " Black Boy " for the big race because he has seen a small negro the day before is not so wildly foolish after all. It is possible, just dimly possible, that the real pattern and scheme of life is not in the least apparent on the outward surface of things, which is the world of common sense, and rationalism, and reasoned deductions ; but rather lurks, half hidden, only apparent in certain rare lights, and then only to the prepared eye ; a secret pattern, an ornament which seems to have but little relation or none at all to the obvious scheme of the universe. Sometimes, in talking to my friends the Spiritualists, I urge on them that one reason for my disbelief in their message is my conviction that the two levels of life, the life here and the life of the world to come, are so utterly distinct. I have read, or rather dipped into, so many books which represent the spirits and souls of the dead as simply continuing their life in this world under conditions which are practically reproductions. The young man who on earth was interested in the affairs of the Mount Zion Chapel (Particular Baptist), Beulah Road, Tooting Bec, is still vividly interested in the pious activities of the old congregation. He communicates with his poor father to that effect: nay, he carries on the old controversies, and points out that Deacon Plinge is, no doubt, convinced by this time as to his error in holding that Moses had the Promise. Nay, if the people on my side went in for these odd orgies, I am sure that it would be just the same. We should have messages about the *Epiclesis* and the *Jube perferri* and the Ancient Liturgical Use of Incense in the Canon, and the superior spirituality of the Roman (or the Sarum) Rite, and so forth and so forth; not to say anything of the Unitarian doctrine obtained through the mediumship of the wonderful Mrs. Pipps, of Jamaica Plain, Mass., U.S.A. Frankly, I believe in not one single word of it all; and not on any pretence of any logical grounds, for what has logic to say of these matters? What would logic have had to say to the X-Ray hypothesis before it was proven? What would logic have to say to a passage which I wrote (in *The Great God Pan*) in the year 1890? Here it is:

"Suppose that an electrician of to-day were suddenly to perceive that he and his friends have merely been playing with pebbles and mistaking them for the foundations of the world; suppose that such a man saw uttermost space lie open before the current, and words of men flash forth to the sun and beyond the sun into the systems beyond, and the voices of articulate-speaking men echo in the waste void that bounds our thought."

Well; so far as we know, it has not quite come to that yet. I remember that once, to my rage and shame and mortification, when I was a reporter, I had to take a taxi in a vast hurry and post off to Greenwich Observatory to ask the Astronomer Royal whether he thought that the Cavaliere Marconi was really receiving messages from Mars. It has not quite come to that yet; but it seems to me that the passage from *The Great God Pan* is a distinct prophecy of " Wireless"; and what would logic have said to it, in 1890, when that chapter was written? I use the word " logic," I may say, in the popular sense, well aware that it is an utterly erroneous one; but as friendly charwomen say when discussing these points, or deeper ones, " you know what I mean." Everything is a miracle before it happens: the reasoning faculties have nothing to say in the presence of the unknown. And it is an odd thing, by the way, that certain propositions which forty years ago would have moved the " scientific " people to mad mirth, which are now commonplaces of everyday demonstration, would have been heard with interest and respect, if not with instant acquiescence, in the early seventeenth century. If a learned German, bearing a name horribly Latinised, had published a treatise in 1615 or thereabouts, showing how there was an art by which the words of a man speaking in Nuremberg might be heard, instantly, in Grand Cairo, nobody would have laughed. The matter would have been discussed : the old Aristotelians would have brought their abstract principles to bear upon it ; the new Baconian school, I think, would have denied the possibility of such a thing ; the Paracelsists and the Rosicrucians would have said that it was highly probable that such an art existed. But the proposition would have been discussed seriously. But ; if the lady sitting next to Huxley at an 1870 dinner table had hinted at the possibility of such an achievement, that most amiable and excellent man would have sipped his claret and looked whimsical ; wondering who had put such wild nonsense into a pretty woman's head. We know now that he would have been wrong ; and, really, it is not a very profound axiom : we know nothing of matters concerning which we know nothing. And so this applies to the

THE LONDON ADVENTURE

ghostly world—always allowing that there is any such world. What do we know ? For all we can say, poor Raymond Lodge and his companions may still be sipping those synthetic whiskies-and-sodas and ætherised cigars by the gates of the New Jerusalem. Who is bold enough to say that it cannot be ? Not I : but I am bold enough to say that it is not so.

For ; I firmly believe that the two worlds have that gulf between them, that *magnum* chaos, which yawns, let us say, between painting and music. You may make analogies between the two arts ; you can talk of the " colour " of this composition or that, just as you may talk of the " colour " of words : but, at last literature, music, painting remain worlds apart. So, I humbly venture to believe, it may be with respect to our life here and our life hereafter. There are relations between the two ; just as there are relations between the life of an actor on the stage and off the stage. But the man who plays the Fool in " Lear " admirably, is not rewarded by instant promotion to the crown of Britain in place of Lear or King George (whom God preserve !). He has his reward : but it is after a different mode. It may run to a flat in one of the best parts of the West End, a charming old house on Romney Marsh, a

French cook of admirable skill, the society of dukes, to the means of bestowing excellent and ample charity or—to anything, indeed, but not to anything connected with the antique Britain of King Lear. The two worlds are related and yet utterly apart ; and so, perhaps, it is with us, and our two worlds ; this world, and the world to come.

For, if we think of it, the antique Britain of Shakespeare's play is more than non-existent. It doesn't exist now ; but it never has existed. It was first an old tradition, an ancient tale told about friendly winter fires on the mountains of wild Wales. It became a printed legend ; a bit of pseudo-history : at last it grew into one of the many vast, enchanted dreams of the greatest master of letters. And so at last Smith plays the Fool in the magnificent West End production of " King Lear " and plays so well that he founds his fortune and can be sure of his two hundred a week or more and all that is implied therein—but not of the pettiest piece of promotion in the Britain of King Lear. And so, perhaps, it may turn out that this world of ours is but one of the dreams of the Supreme Artist. The moon in the sky may be just such an illusion as the moon which the master-electrician causes to rise so convincingly

THE LONDON ADVENTURE

over the dusky garden. The storms of life—hailstorms and fire-showers as Carlyle called them—which beat upon us with such savage fury may, in reality, hurt us just as much as they hurt the actors who are playing Lear and Kent and the Fool in Act III, Scenes 1 and 2.

" Blow, winds, and crack your cheeks! rage! blow! "

and the rest of it : but you will not find these good fellows any the worse for the storm in the dressing-room a little later, or unable to relish their supper at the Garrick or the Green Room a little later still. For, you see, there was no storm ; and so, likely enough, with us ; there is no storm, and stage lightning cannot hurt anybody. Though, of course—to keep up the analogy—the quality of the meat and drink afterwards, when the stage-manager has rung down and the stage is dark may depend entirely on the skill with which we played our parts on the Heath, amidst all those sulphurous and thought-executing fires.

It is this sense, then, of the probable order of things at large that disinclines me to listen to the amiable Conandoylery that is now in such fashion in certain quarters. And, at the same time, it inclines me to believe that very high messengers—in the play, in the mystery which we are enacting—may be quite ordinary fellows in private life, or " off," as the actors would say. How very absurd it would be, if one of the Traitors in " Henry V " on being told by the King to get him gone, poor miserable wretch, unto his doom, were to reply : " I shall do nothing of the kind. You must have had onions with your tea to-night, and your collar was thick with grease-paint on Derby platform last Sunday ; so on the whole I prefer to stay where I am." These very serious accusations may be perfectly well grounded ; but they are impertinent in the proper sense of the word. It is not for us to laugh at the message, because the messengers don't wear their dalmatics in Fleet Street taverns or show a glory about them. Indeed, if one thinks of it, such a course would attract an undesirable amount of attention.

This has been a little digression—I am afraid that there may be one or two more little digressions in the course of this work—designed to show that one should hear and weigh all sorts of messages delivered in all sorts of places. And so I attended with respect and awe to the message that came to me in the tavern in " the Wood " this spring :

" The leaves are beginning to come out."

II

I THINK I have described myself as shuddering, in the Young Man in Spectacles manner, when I received the message about the coming forth of the leaves. But, really, I do not know why I should have shuddered. I had chosen the scheme for the book that was to be written myself ; and I must still pronounce it to be a most excellent scheme. Moreover, I had thought of an excellent title. I was to call my book *The London Adventure*. It was only the other day that I thought I had found out that another man had used this title two or three years before me. *Pereant illi qui ante nos nostra dixerunt.* For I cannot part with my beloved Latin tags, as dark with antiquity and as well-worn as old farmhouse furniture. I love a friendly tag and shall continue to do so, in spite of a stern judge, " D.F.G.", who wrote about another book of mine in the *Boston Evening Transcript*:

"The whole book (*Things Near and Far*) shows the

reflections of a conceited man of mediocre ability, who buries his talent in the ashes of the past, mumbles over it incessant Latin quotations, pats himself on the back because he knows so much Latin to quote and then—is continually irritated because the world hurries by without digging into the ashes, or listening respectfully to his incantations."

In spite of this grave man I shall continue to mumble: though I wish that the tags were not dropping one by one out of my memory; though I wish that I had still the profound Latin scholarship that I possessed as a small boy in the Lower Fourth at Hereford Cathedral School in 1875; when I could grapple with any question relating to *Mensa*, or even, if you liked to push matters to extremities, would run through *amo* with any man alive.

But as to this plan of mine, that was to turn into a book to be called *The London Adventure*. It originated in old rambles about London, rambles that began in 1890 when I lived in Soho Street and began to stroll about Soho and to see that here was something very curious and impressive; this transmutation of late seventeenth-century and early eighteenth-century social solidity and even, in some cases

THE LONDON ADVENTURE

magnificence, into a wholly different order. You turned down this street or that or the other, and you saw, at the foot of it, let us say, a house that had evidently stood in its day for something and somewhat. In the balance of its windows, flush with the walls, there was a certain symmetry and simplicity ; and so about the doorway, its approach of steps, its pillars and its pediment. True ; the matter was London brick, but here you could see the survival of the antique classic tradition, worthily embodied, though not in Parian marble. Here, you could say, once lived a man who played a great part in a great world, whose wig fell great about his shoulders, who sometimes wore a blue ribbon across his deep gold-laced waistcoat when he went abroad. Or perhaps an Ambassador : a Venier, representing the Most Serene Republic of Venice ? But his Embassy was in Soho Square, opposite Mrs. Cornely's establishment. Here, at all events, was an ancient and a dignified house, dim with age ; and you drew near and found that it had become ? Perhaps a Pickle Factory, perhaps a Lithographic Printer's works, perhaps brass labels under half a dozen bells told of as many crafts plied within, or perhaps it was like the Soho house where Newman Noggs lived : a camping ground for poor people, a place where almost every room sheltered a family. Now all this interested me, and so I poked about and mooned about in Soho instead of doing honest work, and speculated as to its narrow alleys and its archways and houses, and its sudden alarums and excursions. For I remember going down Greek Street on a summer afternoon; instantly, without any reason that I could see, a crowd began to pour and buzz from all backways and hidden places and to gather in front of a house which looked as if it had been built for a Doctor of Divinity, *c.* 1720. Then people came down from the doorstep carrying queer objects with them which they bundled into a four-wheeler, and the crowd hummed with delight.

"Pore things," I heard a stout lady say to a stouter friend—both came straight out of Phiz's illustration of Kingsgate Street in *Martin Chuzzlewit* —" pore things: I daresay if the truth was known they only did it for the sake of their wives and families."

And then three or four men were brought out and bundled into another cab, and both cabs drove off. The crowd lounged away, with an expression that seemed to say that there would be a rarer smack

THE LONDON ADVENTURE

about the gin than was common. I went into the post office—I think, but I am not sure, that the golden arm and hammer of the goldbeaters hung over it—and bought some stamps. The postmistress wore ringlets and black silk. She looked as if she had lived all her days in Uttoxeter, Tutbury, Tewkesbury, or Shaftesbury. And yet as she discussed the raid on the German waiters' gambling club—that was what I had seen—there was a certain complacency in her voice, a certain twinkle of a smile on her face, as she said severely :

" Really ! This neighbourhood is getting too dreadful ! "

I believe, in her very heart, she was proud of Greek Street, Soho. At all events things happened there.

Such were the beginnings and first elements of my London science, unless I were to take account of earlier wanderings in the 'eighties, when I roamed out north and west and saw the red brick villas and streets of shops gaining on the quiet fields and old lanes overhung with trees that then made a veritable countryside within ten minutes of Acton. But in writing this book of mine I was to dip rather into the later years ; into the 1895-99 period when I first found out the wonders that lie to the eastward of the Gray's Inn Road, when Islington and Barnsbury and Canonbury were discovered, when Pentonville ceased to be a mere geographical expression. And there was a later time still that was to yield fresh fruit; the days when I ran errands that were often in themselves of inconceivable folly, but led me all the same into queer outland territories that otherwise I should never have seen. I remember once that in the war days I was told to go to Enfield and taste the newly brewed Government ale—some horrible teetotal concoction of those bad times. I had got the names of the taverns where this choice beverage was to be enjoyed, and I took train to Enfield from York Road, King's Cross. Outside Enfield Station I enquired for the public-houses on my list, and was met by the flat information that they were all of them about four miles away; they were not at Enfield at all, but at Enfield Lock. By some complicated process of tram and 'bus and walking I reached the Lock, and found that no one of my pubs knew anything whatever about the new drink, and so my journey was somewhat of a failure. But it was not a failure for me. I had passed through such unsuspected countries in my voyage and travel from

THE LONDON ADVENTURE

Enfield through Enfield Wash to Enfield Lock, through fragments of market garden and fragments of wild thicket, by sudden apparitions of grey houses built in the early 'sixties when it had dawned upon the mind of some madman that the day of the Wash was at hand and that the time for " development " had come. These houses appeared with an awful unexpectedness ; these settlements, of, say, half a dozen houses calling themselves Highsounding Terrace, 1860, manifestly supposing themselves in the first place to be but the nucleus of a whole town of thronging streets, and now standing up a grey island in the desolations of the Wash ; waste lands and raspberry bushes and cabbages all about them. And now and again there would be a corner shop : a fortune was no doubt to be realised by the bold adventurer who would wait a few months, and then be ready to supply the thronging thousands with pickles, tea, cooked meat, and candles : here was the shop ready at the corner, prepared, at the point of vantage. Alas ! there was a corner, but nothing but a corner ; nothing but sodden fields all around. And then, again, a little onward a remnant of much older days : a Georgian mansion, of the seventeen-seventies or thereabouts, built of grey brick with plaster decorations in the manner of the brothers Adam ; with its wall about it and its pillars adorned with grave urns at the entrance gate. There a substantial man,. maybe an Alderman, had once lived ; now, everything was falling down, broken, discoloured, desolate, uninhabited. And the next turn, very likely, would show a very recent error. In 1900, perhaps even in 1910, a modern optimist had arisen and had convinced himself that a vast industrial population must soon be established in the land. He had built a bright red shop and there was a Butcher found to come and open it ; but I cannot conjecture as to where his customers lived. Their houses were not in sight. And so forth and so on. And while I journeyed back to the office, I felt that I had been enjoying a rich and various experience.

And here let me point out that the point of view is totally removed from the ordinary tourist, guidebook point of view. I hope I am not without a due sense of the historic and literary interests of London, with which the guide and the guide-book are very properly occupied. I have my relish for the Temple and the Tower, St. Bartholomew's Church, Staple Inn, for the remnants of the Marshalsea ; and it is a

THE LONDON ADVENTURE

keen relish, too. But that is quite a different matter. That is partly a matter of literary and historical association, of the love of antiquity for its own sake ; a curiously compounded pleasure. And I have remarked that the more noble, terrible, notorious the associations called up, the less I am moved, in my heart of hearts. Honestly, I have grave difficulties over Westminster Abbey, for example. Perhaps, because the Abbey has been the text for so many discourses, because it is one of the great commonplaces of England, and because *difficile est proprie communia dicere*. Perhaps, also, because, as I believe, the surfaces of its stones are not really old English but early Victorian, so that one gazes rather at an image and spectre of a church than at the very church itself. In a sense, therefore, Westminster Abbey is a sham antique ; whereas the old Bell Inn in Holborn was a true antique, as the George in Southwark still is.

But, I confess that this love of antiquity for its own sake, apart from any particular literary or historical associations, has always been a great puzzle to me and still remains so. That high, grim wall of the Marshalsea, for example. I do not suppose that it is by any means of great antiquity ;

THE LONDON ADVENTURE

it is certainly not beautiful ; but perhaps one may justify one's interest in looking at it by the plea of " Little Dorrit "—who never existed. And, by the way, why should we be interested in places more or less connected with the fortunes of people who never existed, outside the brains and the pages of the romancers ? I do not know why we are thus interested, but I know that we are so and that this interest constitutes one of the gentlest of the pleasures of life. I confess, frankly, that when I go to Tower Hill I think much more of the residence of Mr. and Mrs. Quilp in that quarter than of the tremendous and awful events that happened there in stern fact. The dreadful end of actual traitors moves me much less than the thought of that " mixed tea, new bread, fresh butter, shrimps, and water-cresses " which were consumed with such a relish by the creatures of Dickens's brain, in the shady, lazy room with a view of the old Tower. So it is ; and here, it seems to me, is one of the minor enigmas of life. There never was a Mrs. Quilp, she didn't live on Tower Hill and she never gave a tea-party in the room which she never occupied : what a wonder it is that all this fiction should be so much more impressive—to some minds—than solid and

THE LONDON ADVENTURE

majestic fact. For me, Anne Boleyn, Lady Jane Grey, and all the " traitors " who passed into the Tower and perished awfully there are as mere shadows compared with Mr. Quilp, Mrs. Quilp, and that most engaging old lady, Mrs. Jiniwin. Perhaps, the explanation may be that the historic people are actual people, creatures of fact not of fancy ; and that fancy is infinitely more impressive than fact, partaking, as it does, not of actuality, but of reality. In a certain sense, it is probable that Mr. Micawber is more real than any of us, infinitely more real than Dickens's own father, of whom he is understood to be a glorified projection. I once asked a Sheffield man if he would be so good as to give me a definition of steel. " Certainly," said he. " Steel is simply iron freed from all the other substances which are found associated with it." We are all of us associated with " other substances " ; it is only the beings of true literature who are pure and without alloy, since their essences are simple and immortal.

But to return to the—more or less—chief topic of this discussion : the book that I was to write, the book to be called *The London Adventure*, was not to deal in the main with the historical or literary associations of London, nor even with antiquity as such, though sometimes antiquity would form part of the queer pattern that I had in my mind. For instance : the grey Georgian house with its solemn urns and mouldering ornaments fell into its place in the story of the journey from Enfield to Enfield Lock : but not from the artistic or antiquarian standpoint. It was part of the general queerness ; a piece, a *tessera*, that fitted in very pleasantly with that hopeless 1860 terrace and that desolate 1900 shop, and the cabbages, and the raspberry plantations and, above all and before all, with the sense that I had never been that way before, that the scene to me was absolutely new and unknown, as if the African Magician had suddenly set me down in the midst of Cathay, that I was as true an explorer as Columbus, as he who stood upon a peak in Darien. For if you think of it : the fact that the region which is to you so strange and unknown is familiar as daily bread and butter or—more likely—the lack of it to multitudes of your fellow-men is of no significance on earth. I think that the first land that Columbus saw when he had made his incredible adventure of the Atlantic was one of the West India Islands. Well : you can imagine how awfully and splendidly

THE LONDON ADVENTURE

that dimness on the verge of the sea struck upon his soul : but it was common enough, I suppose, to the Carib Indians who lived on it ; and to the Mexicans and Peruvians and the other tribes their course of life was as natural, accustomed and uninteresting as an At Home in South Kensington or a Chapel Tea in Dorchester are to the inhabitants of those agreeable regions. Montezuma, if I remember, and I remember these things very vaguely, had a special robe or headdress of feathers of some extremely rare bird. Very likely ; but in itself that is no more amazing than the feather stoles which ladies carry now, no more wonderful in itself than the miniature of my grandfather, the Vicar of Caerleon, which my grandmother wore as a brooch. In Mexico you wore a feather robe ; in Caerleon you wore black silk and a painted likeness of your husband as a fastening to it; in Peru the Government accounts were kept on strings with knots on them ; in England they were kept, till recent days, on bits of stick with notches on them. It seems clear to me that nothing exists vitally, that is, as an object of wonder, surmise, awe, exultation, or mirth in itself. I write with all submission to Holy Church ; but it appears that in the world of profane things, at all events, there are no sacraments *ex opere operato*. Are we not all in the same boat ? I have just been listening to the *Agnus Dei* from Bach's great Mass in B Minor. I am assured, on the best authority, that it is magnificent : to me it is a disagreeable noise. Voltaire thought the works of Shakespeare a form of mania ; Smollett, a very acute man, had exactly the same opinion of York Minster—he said it was a pity they did not build a " neat Grecian room " in place of the Cathedral ; and a French gentleman of my acquaintance told me how he had once eaten roast lamb with " sauce menthe." " Je n'aimais pas ça," he said, with eloquent simplicity, meaning, I am sure, that he found the combination barbarous and disgusting ; as I should find the Christmas dish of Germany, carp boiled in beer, disgusting and barbarous. It seems, then, I say ; that nothing in the natural order is of itself, or absolutely ; that to A. a little stucco villa of 1830 with a green verandah and a green latticed porch will give more pleasure than St. Paul's or Canterbury Cathedral affords to B.—just as Mrs. Quilp and her friends do me much more good than Anne Boleyn and *her* friends. And I confess that this conclusion tends to persuade me very strongly in favour of a former argument : that the storms of life are no more real than the storms of the stage, which depend on " Props." King Lear is not in the least dead : he is enjoying a mixed grill at his club. The Duke who had his eyes put out can see perfectly well and is regulating the admixture of soda and " spot " with clear and admirable vision. The play is a play indeed ; but it is a play within a play, which we call life, which is also unreal, though after a different mode of being. And so I say that there is no such entity as the thing in itself, there is no absolute existence in things seen ; and, against my own feelings, that even the rawest, reddest modern suburb, with those shops that are the same everywhere, with those villas that are the same everywhere, with that terrible, victorious invasion of green woods and peaceful lawns—more awful in a way, perhaps, than the German invasion of France—that even these vile, red stones may be transmuted into living, philosophical stones ; as Robertus de Fluctibus has it. Here, if you will, even in these places, you can conjecture the sighs of the victim, the rapture of the priest ; here the mysteries are celebrated, even as in Eleusis ; the ritual is duly performed, though those who officiate are ignorant of the secrets in which they, nevertheless, share. I have always thought it a singular and curious thing that Freemasonry—in its essentials a most ancient rite—should still exist among us and exist vigorously, and be a high, important, respectable institution, patronised by Royalty, the right thing to belong to, as fine a thing in its way as the Church of England, by law established. The Freemasonry of to-day has, of course, been " reformed " like the other institution which I have mentioned ; nobody, perhaps, quite knows what happened to it in the early 'twenties of the eighteenth century. Many things were removed, many things obscured ; still the heart of the mystery remained, and remains still. And no doubt there are Freemasons, nay, many Freemasons, who know, more or less, what they are doing ; but the vast majority of the Craft are certainly very little aware that they are celebrating the rites of an ancient mystery religion, originating, so far as the west is concerned, about the first century of our era, a contemporary, in fact, of Christianity itself. I remember that once in my newspaper days I had to see a brassfounder in Clerkenwell. My business with him was connected with a Ghost of a very singular kind ; but I filled up an interval in our proper conversation with an enquiry as to the process of his business.

" Is brass cast in the old way ? " I asked. " Or have all sorts of new methods and processes been introduced ? "

" Brass," he replied, " is cast now as it always has been cast ; as it was cast when the columns of brass were made gloriously for the Temple of King Solomon."

" I know the name of the man who did that casting," was my answer. " And I know what happened to him."

My brassfounder looked at me.

" Are you on the square ? " said he.

I said I was sorry, but I wasn't on the square ; and we resumed our enquiry into a particular instance of that other ancient and insoluble mystery, the Poltergeist, which had been manifesting in a northern suburb. Now here was an intelligent and fervent Mason, but how little he realised that his Father in the Craft was much more than a Brassfounder, much more than a Master Builder, that he belonged to a race removed from man, and that his true name was, very possibly, Sabazius : that he was, perhaps, of the house of Osiris ? I think this good

Son of the Widow knew little of all this; and so, as I say, with the vast majority of the brethren. Yet, the ancient rite is duly performed, and so other ancient rites are performed in the rawest, reddest suburbs, as I once tried to declare in a story called *The Fragment of Life.* There are, unhappily, in these days, people who profane these holy mysteries, some of them calling themselves, I am told, psychoanalysts, others professing a high-souled enthusiasm for the physical good of the race. And I believe that Coventry Patmore, if he had lived into our unhappy days and had seen these things would have cursed the new profanation even more than he cursed the old; which is generally known as the Protestant Reformation. Patmore might have said, I think, that if the well-springs of nature were poisoned, if the water were turned into sewage; could even Grace transmute such water as that into Wine? The Miracle of Cana is a great wonder, doubtless, and a great symbol; but true miracles never contradict and defy nature; they rather restore nature to its first and unfallen state. Eyes are meant to see with: consequently the blind were given their sight. But if the waterpots of Cana had been full, not of water, but of liquid manure?

THE LONDON ADVENTURE

Well ; I was saying, I think, that the book on hand, this famous *London Adventure*, would have to deal with the raw, red places all around the walls of London ; places detestable in themselves, no doubt, from the artist's point of view, from the point of view of the lover of green fields and woods and shady lanes ; but most of all detestable, I think, from my point of view, which is that of a man who loves ancient, memoried things ; things of all kinds that have a past behind them, things of all kinds that show use and the touch of men upon them, and have become, in a sense, almost human or, at all events, partake of humanity. I can look with a kind of pleasure on a very doorstep, on a doorstep approaching a shabby grey house of 1810 or thereabouts—if the stone be worn into a deep hollow by the feet of even a hundred years and a little over. That poor London stone in the back-street off the Gray's Inn Road, is in its very minor way, a *Lapis ex cælis*—for I cannot accept my friend A. E. Waite's interpretation of the Lapis Exillit of Wolfram von Eschenbach. The feet of the weary and hopeless, the glad and the exultant, the lustful and the pure have made that hollow ; and most of those feet are now in the hollow of the grave : and that doorstep is to me sacramental, if not a sacrament, even though the neighbourhood round about Mount Pleasant is a very poor one. For, it seems to me that here you have the magic touch which redeems and exalts the dull mass of things, by tinging them with the soul of man. What was that doorstep in the rough, in the rock, but a chunk of limestone, matter for the geologist or the roadmender, possibly, but for no one else? It is an instance, at the very bottom of the ladder, of the high miracle of veritable architecture, of Canterbury, Lincoln, Durham. Here you have, in fact, in the fact of the geologist, simply great heaps of stone dug out of the earth, and piled up on top of it. But the hand of man has so worked upon these rough masses, has so grouped them and carved them and carried them towards the skies, that you see the miracle of the dead raised to life, of the dull and shapeless mass informed with the living spirit. And —it is a lesser art, I admit freely—I see those worn and hollowed doorsteps round about Clerkenwell and the Gray's Inn Road and all the dim and desolate regions adjacent; I see them signed with tears and desires, agony and lamentation; and perhaps on those stones have stood the feet of those who have witnessed the Operation of the Great Work, and have seen the Son Blessed of the Fire. For strange lodgers sometimes take up their abode in quite shabby houses, in undesirable neighbourhoods.

My book, then, was to take all these things into account : the old, the shabby, the out of the way ; and also the new and the red and the raw. But it was utterly to shun the familiar. For if you think of it, there is a London *cognita* and a London *incognita*. We all know about Piccadilly and Oxford Street, London Bridge and the Strand. Olympia has made us familiar with a little island in otherwise unknown Hammersmith ; the Boat Race illuminates Putney, and the most inexperienced have ventured into the High Street, Kensington. But where will you be, if I ask you about Clapton, about the inner parts of Barnsbury, about the delights of Edmonton; about that region which was once called Spa Fields ? Nay : how many people know their Camden Town in any thorough and intelligent manner ? They may know the main artery of it by which the omnibuses go up to Hampstead ; but not the byways, not the curious passages of Camden Town into Holloway. I remember once; I think it must have been in this borderland between the two quarters, coming at haphazard upon an unpretending street that to me was a whole chapter in social history. The houses were modest little places enough, standing back from the road, houses for small incomes, one would say. But each one of them had its little coach-house and its little stable; and for me here were compact histories of the *Sketches by Boz* period. Here lived, I suppose, people of the £250-£350 a year standard, as money was in those days. I conceive them as living quite carefully. There would be one little maid who did the rougher work of the house, who got up very early indeed in the morning and swept the rooms and lit the fires. But the mistress, or perhaps a daughter, helped her to make the beds and very likely—see Miss Trotwood—washed up the real china cups and saucers, and was responsible for the cakes and the tarts and all the niceties of cookery. The boy or hobbledehoy who looked after the pony and the basket-work chaise for six pounds a year, blacked the boots and did all sorts of odd jobs about the house and garden. I should suppose there were two joints of meat a week, but no more. There were eggs for breakfast, but no bacon. If master were " retired," then the principal meal of the day was between one and three of the

THE LONDON ADVENTURE

afternoon : otherwise the boy, the pony and the chaise took him into the City in the morning and brought him back to dinner in the evening. The gig and pony were sometimes put up in dim stable yards and back places, the very site and existence of which, in our modern London, must remain a profound mystery ; and what the boy did in the interval, between morning and evening I cannot imagine. Perhaps, even probably, he drove back to Camden Town and cleaned knives and worked in the garden till five o'clock, and then set out again to fetch the master. Sometimes he would drive his mistress to Hornsey where Cousin Jane lived. Then master would walk back from the City and think nothing of it. It was all a very small life. On the sideboard— Sheraton, very likely, for people of slight means could not afford to buy smart modern furniture— there were cake and wine ; sherry wine and port wine—ready for anybody, who might pay a morning call ; but in the absence of such visitors, I do not think that the mistress of the house or her daughters often partook of these dainties. The cake, I daresay, was apt to get somewhat dry and the wine to grow somewhat flat and weary before the sentence was uttered : " We may as well finish them." Three or four times a year the family started early in the morning and drove off to Twickenham to see Uncle James, who was well to do. There was roast veal or goose for dinner, veal and ham pie or beefsteak pudding, Scotch Ale and Madeira. There might be salmon, there might be pheasant—according to the season—and if there were any sort of family anniversary, champagne might well be produced. If it were warm weather, the men of the party spent an hour or two of the afternoon in the summer-house overlooking the river, drinking punch. The ladies did their "work" in the drawing-room and told family histories. At ten o'clock, after a bowl of bishop and a sandwich with the alternative of tea and thin bread and butter, the bell was rung, the boy was ordered to put in the pony, and the party returned to Camden Town. There was probably, almost certainly "something hot" before going to bed; and this also was the case after one of the rare visits to the play. These people took no regular summer holidays; now and again they stayed for a week or two with relations in Somerset, and that was all, and in return, a son or a daughter of the relations in Somerset would stay for a week in the house in Camden Town, and for that week the family budget would be swollen. There would be ham for breakfast, something extra in the pudding way for dinner, a couple of theatres in the week, and oysters for supper afterwards, instead of the usual bread and cheese. Very few books in that house : odd volumes of Pope, Akenside, Smollett, The Rambler, Don Quixote, Drelincourt on Death, Law's Serious Call ; none of them much read.

So much I saw as I passed down that street, Camden Town—Holloway, and I believe that most of it is truly seen ; deduced rather, from the little coach-houses and the little stables ; and all a vision of a mode of life that has passed utterly away.

But ; I have just remembered. I was speaking of the Clerkenwell Brassfounder and his connection with a certain singular enquiry which brought us together for a brief season. I must not be too explicit, but while I tarried in Clerkenwell and met the metal workers at their taverns, I heard some curious things about an old London family, established in an ancient craft in that part for a hundred and fifty years and perhaps more. It is a modern superstition that all Londoners are, *qua* Londoners, things of recent date ; that either they or their fathers came up to town from Inverness or Falmouth, Cromer or Pembroke. This is true enough, perhaps, of ourselves and of the Londoners that we know; but down below, beneath our cognisance of things, there is still the old town, the settled place, and the hereditary crafts, as if it were Cirencester or Wootton Bassett. Well, seated in the Clerkenwell Tavern, between the Brassfounder and a man who, I think, was interested in aluminium—or " ally," as he called it—I heard some odd tales of the race I have mentioned.

" There was the great-uncle," said the aluminium specialist. " He was a strange man. He wanted to spite his relations—I forget what it was all about. So he took three hundred pounds in gold, and put them in a pot and buried them. And there they were, till the navvies came to make the cutting for the Midland Railway and found the money."

" He was a very odd man from what they say," said the Brassfounder. " So was his cousin. He confuted Darwin."

" Really ! " I interjected. " Surely not."

" Oh, yes, he did," confirmed the dealer in aluminium. " He proved that Darwin was all wrong by the Hebrew Alphabet—and by the stars."

THE LONDON ADVENTURE

" Yes ; that was what *he* did," and thus the Brass-founder ended the discussion. But, as an afterthought :

" And I wish you'd get your paper to let us have the metal prices day by day ; we should find them very useful."

And this was only an interlude in the real business which had brought us together. This, as I have said, was an affair of the Poltergeist, which had been raising sad havoc in a house of one of the remoter northern suburbs. The quarter, which I shall not specifically name, lest worthy people, who were horribly annoyed and distressed at the time, should be annoyed yet more, was one of those which still happily linger about us, and more especially in the northern parts of London. Happily, I say, because in spite of the rows and rows of cheap red villas, which we must expect everywhere, there are still remnants of a former age. There was the old parish church, not really of noble architecture, but deeply draped in dark green ivy and wearing somehow a venerable air, standing in the old churchyard on the side of the hill, with grave elms about it. Perhaps Edgar Allan Poe was at school not far from here, in the days when these northern suburbs could be justly described as " dreamy villages." Then, there was the principal inn of the place, an eighteenth-century building, " done up," of course, but not done up too much ; and in the main street, here and there, midst the flaunting, flaring shops, a quiet house of the time of Queen Anne stood back amidst trees and lawns and flowers in a green and peaceful retirement from the jingle of the road. Then, of course, a stretch of brisk, bright shopkeeping, as up to date as you please ; and perhaps in the middle of the red bricks and the plate glass a humble little gabled cottage, a remnant of the sixteenth century, somehow surviving into an age of progress. When I see such places, I always hope that the occupant and owner is a cantankerous and consistent old woman, who tells speculative builders and " developers " and estate agents exactly what she thinks of them. And here and there, in the side streets, the back gardens of the rubbishy little red houses still give on the fields and are bordered by trees of old growth.

It was in such a neighbourhood, then, that I was to investigate the doings of the Poltergeist ; the rackety spirit. The afflicted family consisted of two elderly married people, their two sons, an aunt, and three grandchildren, a little girl of five and two boys of, say, nine and eleven. The story was the usual story. The grandmother, or the aunt, would be quietly cooking in the kitchen of an evening. Suddenly there was a crash ; the window was broken and a lump of coal and some fragments of glass would be found in the garden outside. I saw the jagged holes in the kitchen window, and the glass and the coals outside. I saw glass and china which had been smashed, as I was told, in other rooms of the house. I talked to the various members of the family, who struck me as honest people in very considerable distress at these occurrences. I talked to the clergyman of the church which some of them attended. I had been told that he had been an actual witness of some of the " phenomena " ; he had seen, I think, some mantelpiece ornament shooting from its place and dropping on the floor on the other side of the room. I found that he was firmly convinced of the supernatural origin of these strange events. I asked him :

" Did you actually see that ash-tray—or whatever it was—shoot off the mantelpiece, fly across the room and drop on the floor ? "

He asked me another :

" Do you see the ball at Lord's all through its

course, from the moment that it touches the bat to the moment that it touches the ground?"

In short, I tried to make head and tail of the story. I made neither; I made nothing of it at all. I have said that the family struck me as an honest family. They had certainly nothing to gain by having their possessions—to the value of three or four pounds, I believe—smashed to pieces. And when the business became known through the agency of my colleagues and myself, they had still less to gain; for every night a noisy mob packed itself into their quiet, forsaken road and pressed at their gate, and howled at their windows. A number of journalists —I was not one of them—passed the night in the house and saw nothing and heard nothing. The little girl grandchild died; and I daresay the poor child's end was hastened, though not caused, as I gathered, by all the turmoil, within the house and without it. And the last I heard of the whole matter was, that one of the boys had suddenly become a victim to epileptic fits. And so the whole story passes into nothingness and oblivion, and presently, in a year or three years or five years, just such a tale comes from the neighbourhood of the Wash, or the High Wolds of Yorkshire; the

THE LONDON ADVENTURE

scene a lonely farm instead of a small suburban house ; and again the eager reporters rush to the spot ; and again—there is nothing ; no result, neither confirmation nor refutation. I wrote the whole story in a tale of mine called *The Great Return ;* six years before I had any actual experience of the matter. Thus :

"Now and then such doings as these excite a whole neighbourhood ; sometimes a London paper sends a man down to make an investigation. He writes half a column of description on the Monday, a couple of paragraphs on the Tuesday, and then returns to town. Nothing has been explained, the matter vanishes away ; and nobody cares. The tale trickles for a day or two through the Press, and then instantly disappears, like an Australian stream, into the bowels of darkness."

And that is exactly what happens. It happened in that affair of the Northern suburb which I was sent to investigate. Of course, I could investigate nothing. I listened to what I was told, I saw the smashed windows and the broken crockery and the lumps of coal ; but that is nothing. The only person who can investigate the Poltergeist properly will be a member of the afflicted household with an open mind and keen and open eyes, without prepossessions on one side or the other. There are all sorts of difficulties to be encountered. I remember that in one of the articles which I wrote on the particular case which we have been discussing, I said that there was always a young person, a young boy or a young girl, in the Poltergeist histories. A correspondent wrote to me in correction. He said that he and his wife and a friend, a man, all of them of thirty years or so, had been annoyed in this manner and had never found any solution of their troubles. And then ; take it that the whole thing is a fraud, the mischievous trick of the adolescent, the effect of the troubled mind in the troubled body. Very well ; but how strange that the methods and ways seem always of the same order. We can hardly suppose that these young people have read up the subject, and simply imitate the mischief of other young people before them. It may be, of course, that it is all " natur'," which we know, on high authorities, to be both a holy thing and a rum 'un. It may be that it is an instinct in young males and females of a certain nervous diathesis to throw things and chunks about with devilish art and cunning, so that everybody is horribly puzzled. This may be so ; but it is very odd, if it be so. It is almost as odd, but not quite so odd, as my own very tentative hypothesis, held with doubt and infinitely subject to correction and refutation : that a human being is a world and cosmos of forces that reach out to other worlds wholly, or almost wholly, unknown and unconjectured ; that, in most cases and probably, as things are, for the best, these forces and powers are dormant and unsuspected ; that occasionally and by accident they assert themselves and produce results which prove—nothing.

There is a scene which is very deeply impressed on my memory. It belongs to the old days of the Road when one wandered up and down England, from squalid manufacturing hamlets to beautiful, ancient and utterly peaceful places. One day the morning stroll was by the green swelling ramparts of the Roman Wall, not far from Hexham ; on the next it might lead us on the black and horrible track of Hetton-le-Hole, where the little brooklet in the valley throws up miniature beaches of coal-dust, where the players, in one instance, had to climb up a sort of step ladder to their bedroom, and then leap over a gulf between the top step of the ladder and the bedroom floor. For the white road of the old players led, and I suppose still leads, to endless variety: to the little Scotch towns of the border, where the language spoken is still almost unintelligible, where the aspect of things is very much that of a somewhat dingy town in the French provinces, an aspect which is further heightened by the fact that the humblest cooking is excellent, and that the fancy cakes in the small confectioners' shops surpass the cakes of Bond Street. And, thence, the road may wind away to Leamington or Cheltenham or Bath, to the ordered, beautiful towns of the eighteenth century. Or it may twist to Lincoln where you find yourself climbing up to the Cathedral by the way which is called Straight, or it may diverge to Tewkesbury with its noble minster and its admirable half-timbered, gabled houses, rich with fifteenth-century carving, or, just as likely, take you to Swansea, where they smelt twenty-two metals, and, on the whole, look like it.

Well, one of the twists and turnings of this famous road, where there is no money but plenty of happiness, took me eighteen years ago or so to the beautiful city of Bath. There was a " night off " —I forget how or why—and a few of us drifted that evening to the rooms of two of the band, there to

THE LONDON ADVENTURE

drink whisky and smoke and talk and laugh in our vicious, abandoned way. The company consisted of two women and three men. Of the two men besides myself one was a middle-aged actor who had played leads for many years in "Number 2" provincial companies; the other was a youngish man, who had been a novice in a great Benedictine monastery, afterwards a student of sculpture in Belgium, and finally had turned to the stage. Well, there we were, spending our pleasant evening together, and I can hardly realise now, after those eighteen years, how with about twopence in our pockets and within a fortnight's notice of destitution—the fortnight's notice may appear on the callboard any night—we laughed at anything and everything and didn't even care that twopence which we somewhat dubiously possessed. And I have often wondered whether it ever struck the Benedictine Novice that there were certain resemblances between the life that he had abandoned—for lack of vocation —and the life which he had adopted. There are of course grave differences and I hope nobody will suspect me of doubting which is the higher calling; but there is this point of likeness : neither the good monk nor the good actor cares twopence ! Each is rooted and fortified and secure : the one in God, the other in gaiety; the gaiety, I suppose, of publicans and sinners.

So, I say, we sat and laughed about the fire, when it occurred to one of the party, the old actor or the novice, I am not sure which, to say :

" Let's have a séance."

I stood out, being generally of Panurge's opinion when any particular course of action is proposed : " It is better to drink." But the other four sat down round a small rosewood table, in the middle of the room, under the flaring gaslights, and did some kind of hanky-panky with fingers and thumbs. I am afraid somebody was profane enough to recite the Pater Noster : the sitting had begun. I stood a few feet away, puffing at my pipe and looking with contemptuous and easy tolerance at the " four idiots," as I regarded them. But I must make it clear that, to the best of my belief, none of the four had any particular notions about spiritualism or knowledge of it : to them it was merely a parlour game, a substitute for poker.

But as I looked I perceived that the features of one of the party were becoming curiously intent, almost contorted, almost rapturously contorted, as with an acute and singular pleasure. I forget whether anything else of an audible or visible kind were going on. I am inclined to think that the former Benedictine in a burlesque voice with a burlesque earnestness addressed " the dear spirits " and implored them to show a friendly temper and to rap or tilt the table ; to do the decent thing in fact. There was no rapping, no tilting. The séance, with one exception, was getting bored, and some sort of a halt was called ; and, I suppose, those fingers and thumbs were unlocked. But the interested member of the party called out in a voice of intense eagerness and excitement, much removed from her ordinary manner : " Oh, let's go on, let's go on " : and the sitting was resumed. And oddly enough, I remember no more, so far as personal observation is concerned. I conjecture that I got tired of looking and had some more whisky and smoked my pipe in a corner armchair in a patient, resigned sort of way, wondering when they would all have done with their nonsense. But afterwards, when it was over, the lady who had seemed so highly interested during the former part of the proceedings, told me that the second stage had been dreadful, so far as she was concerned. A sense of great horror had come upon her, and with that a physical sense as of an icy breath in the little, stuffy, overheated room; and then, last of all, there had been the feeling of a presence, the presence of a dear friend, who had died suddenly some four years before. " Somehow, I felt that poor Blank was there," she said, and the sense of horror—overhaul Job for particulars of that sense—was so great that she very solemnly declared that she would never have anything to do with such matters again, even though it might be all a joke and a parlour game.

Now, I should like to note that being, as I hope, a fair man, I tell this true story, in a sense, against myself. I have no belief in the art of necromancy; I do not think that the spirits of the dead can be conjured into a parlour by people sitting round a table in the dark—or in the light either. Still; I repeat what I was told, and I am sure that the teller of the story told the truth; that is, repeated this particular sensation as it came to her.

And then: there are two important differences between this odd business in the actor's rooms at Bath in the October of 1905 and the real séance of the spiritualists. The four players were not in the least serious. They thought it would be fun, though

I don't quite know what they expected would happen. At the séance proper everybody is entirely serious. They are investigators. They are intensely interested. They have a profound belief that the spirits of the departed can and do communicate with the living. They fervently expect to experience such communication before they rise from the table. With some of the sitters this is a matter of theory and science ; with others, poor people, there is the aching desire to be quite sure that the beloved is not dead but living. In a word, these people are in earnest ; they are not playing a game. There is no wild exaltation. And then secondly, when their desire is realised, as they suppose, there is no trace of horror. There is no sense of the awfulness of another order of being impinging on ours. It is all as cheerful as a tea-party. The spirits are gay, friendly, familiar ; it is just as it was in the old days, when they were alive, in the common sense of the word. You are simply assured that John is still hearty and well, the very same John, with much the same interests as those of the John whom you knew and loved so well, with just the same little family jokes and turns of speech ; and you go home after the séance cheerful and happy.

Well, these seem to me to be notable differences. Though I have told the story truly, as, I am quite certain, it was truly told to me ; I still disbelieve in the presence of the spirit of poor, dead Blank in that actors' lodging-house in Bath. But I think that something happened ; that the doors were opened ; that the human spirit came into momentary contact with unconjectured worlds which it is not meant to visit.

I think of these things as I pass along the interminable wandering of the London streets ; of the strange things which may have been done behind the weariest, dreariest walls.

III

HERE, then, was the situation before me in this spring of the year. The leaves were out, as the dread messenger of the tavern had informed me, the stage of the London scene was fully set, and here was I well equipped with long-gathered material for a sermon on the great text that there is wonder in everything and everywhere, wonder above all in this great town that has grown so vast that no man can know it, nay, nor even begin to know it! I was thinking of a sentence I had written in a book of mine called *Far Off Things* to the effect that no man has ever seen London; and then, wandering a little—I am afraid that " wandering a little " is almost a hobby of mine—I began to consider whether, in this respect, London were the unique matter that I had considered it. For, referring back the axiom to its most august origin : we are ready enough to confess—if we be not occultists, who know everything—that no man hath seen God at any time. But are we prepared to admit that no man hath seen anything at any time? Yet, this is most indubitably the truth. We see appearances and outward shows of things, symbols of all sorts; but we behold no essences, nor could we bear to behold them, if it were possible to do so. We know what happened to the lady in the " haythen mythology," as the hedge-schoolmaster called it, who obtained her desire, that she should see her lover Zeus in his true essence, as Hera saw him. Her wish was fulfilled, and she was blasted and consumed in devouring flame. This is one of the old lies that are so much truer than the new truths; and it is like enough—Tennyson put the matter in a different manner—that if any man could see a grain of wheat as it is in its essence, he would instantly become a raging maniac. We see nothing real, we can no more see anything real than we can take our afternoon tea in the white, central heat of a blast furnace. We see shadows cast by reality. The more foolish of us gather up some of the shadows and put them in saucepans and boil them and then strain : and find out that water is really H_2O, which is true enough in its way, and will remain so : till it is found out that H_2 is shorthand for ten distinct forces, while

THE LONDON ADVENTURE

O is a universe of countless stars, all revolving in their eternal order about an unknown, unconjecturable orb. And this, again, will be a good working hypothesis—till, new discoveries call for an entire revision of all our notions on the subject. No ; we see nothing at all ; though poets catch strange glimpses of reality, now and then, out of the corners of their eyes.

And the recognition of these obvious truths cast me down a little. I had not, then, got the unique object for investigation that I had supposed. London, it was true, was unknowable, an unplumbed depth, but so was Caerleon-on-Usk, that you could see in its totality from the top of the hill ; so was the pebble on the path. I felt I must have a little time to look around me and reconsider the matter ; and while I did so, I thought it would be a good thing to glance through the notebook that I used in 1895, '96, '97, '98 ; in the period when I was writing *The Hill of Dreams, Ornaments in Jade, The White People, A Fragment of Life, Hieroglyphics*. We learn by experience, say the good men ; but I believe the fact to be that experience causes us to forget most things that are worth knowing—as Wordsworth has observed in a somewhat higher manner in his *Ode*.

And so, I said to myself, before I begin this magistral work about London, I will disinter the old notebook, which I kept when I was young, and understood one or two things far more clearly than I do now.

I opened it at random. I came upon what follows. I had utterly forgotten that I had ever written it. I did not know that I had once been clever enough to write gibberish.

> I wish to paint the ardent grace
> That shines upon my Mary's face,
> And speak of that within her eyes
> That sings to me of Paradise.
>
> She came to me from a distant shore,
> She came to me through a secret door;
> And when she walks, I know how they
> Must dance in a secret land alway.
>
> Her locks are scented with spices rare,
> Her Secret is one that no mortals share;
> For she goes ever in a light
> That shines upon no earthly wight.
>
> O Mary, bend to me your eyes,
> Instructing me in mysteries,
> Wherein all joys are found, that I
> Unto this dying life may die;
> And live for ever wrapt in Thee
> O present immortality.

THE LONDON ADVENTURE

This, evidently, was an extract from the notebooks of the young City clerk in *A Fragment of Life*, the " inspired infant " who also wrote the lines beginning:

One day when I was all alone
I found a wondrous little stone.

To those who have not read this story it may be explained that Darnell, the clerk, was a man who " woke up " to real existence, to the sense of things that veritably are ; and, without any education of the technical or formal kind, pottered with old books —he had evidently glanced into Vaughan and Crashaw—and wrote " poems," which, in spite of their rough, ungrammatical, conventional crust— " wight " is rather terrible—yet have a flame burning within them.

I read over the lines again, and thinking over them I was reminded of Henry James's story, *The Pattern on the Carpet ;* the notion of a man of letters who had written many books and was quite surprised to find that one of his admirers had failed to recognise that all these tales of his were variations on one theme ; that a common pattern, like the pattern of an Eastern carpet, ran through them all. If I remember ; the novelist died suddenly, without revealing the nature of the pattern, and James ends very exquisitely, leaving us with the faithful admirer, who, we are to understand, is to pass the rest of his days in endeavouring to penetrate the mystery of this one design, latent in a whole shelf of books.

Well, I read my clerk's doggerel, and thought of the tale of the pattern, and began to wonder a little whether the " poem " did not furnish the key to the pattern of my carpet; nay, I would say to my " Orient carpet, nine by nine, brilliant colours, fifteen and six." " If you go to Dick's in the Seven Sisters Road, mention the name of Mr. Wilson of Fulham and ask for Mr. Johnston." But I was forgetting: all this happened years ago. Dick's now charge you thirty-five and six for the " Orient " carpet and Mr. Johnston is dead. He died violently; but they sent Mrs. Johnston his V.C. and she lives at Waltham Cross, and keeps a small school for very small children.

But I was thinking, as I have said, that here was something like the pattern of my cheap " Orient " square in brilliant colours. For this " Mary," to whom these lines that try to flame were addressed, was quite an ordinary young woman. Before her marriage to Edward Darnell, the City Clerk, she had

THE LONDON ADVENTURE

been Miss Mary Reynolds, the daughter of an estate agent and auctioneer in Notting Hill, an auctioneer in a pretty small way. She was just a pleasant, amiable, conventional young woman, who had considerably more sense than her husband where money matters were concerned, did her best with his very small income, and was continually worried by the kitchen range and by the whims of her servant, Alice. Yet:

> When she walks, I know how they
> Must dance in a secret land alway.

Here, then, is the pattern in my carpet, the sense of the eternal mysteries, the eternal beauty hidden beneath the crust of common and commonplace things; hidden and yet burning and glowing continually if you care to look with purged eyes. Nay, I think that in this age, which has probably lost what I may call the epic sense, as it lives in villas and flats instead of castles, and goes in tweeds in place of chain mail, for us, I think, it is easier to discern the secret beauty and wonder and mystery in humble and common things than in the splendid and noble and storied things. I have been in Avignon, for example, and I hope I did not fail to realise its mystic beauty, as the sunset light glowed on its

THE LONDON ADVENTURE

white machicolated walls. Here was a pure and intact relic from another world, from all the world of the beauty and romance and the music and the singing of old Provence; here was a city that was like the dying echoes of a magistral song. I could see all this and feel it deeply; and yet I was something like the old Japanese poet to whom an Englishman read " In Memoriam." The Japanese understood not one word; but he wept—at the sheer beauty of the sound of the words. And so I, under the walls of Avignon, admired deeply but did not understand. A great music, a great voice, indeed, but not speaking in my native tongue. In one sense, it said a great deal; in another sense it said nothing. Nay, take the example of a man of supreme genius, such as Dickens. He made his tours in France and Italy, and the experience gave him little. The best thing that he got from France was the contrast between railway refreshment rooms in England and France ("Mugby Junction"). There is a very sunny and pleasant chapter on Sens in *Mrs. Lirriper's Legacy;* and, so far as I remember, that is all. Very agreeable, indeed, but not the vital, the tremendous Dickens; not, by any means, the essential Dickens who appears in Pickwick and his

THE LONDON ADVENTURE

companions, in Micawber, and Mrs. Gamp, in Quilp, in the Flora of *Little Dorrit*, in the majestic figure of Mr. F.'s Aunt. Avignon and Rome and Genoa : great places, no doubt, and full of mighty eloquence, but the tongue was foreign, the idiom altogether strange. Charles Dickens was touched to the heart and the quickening spirit not by these, but by Camden Town by-ways, by the old inns of Southwark, by dirty streets in Soho, by the purlieus of the Gray's Inn Road. He understood their utterance, since it was in his native tongue. And so with Hawthorne : " Transformation " is a great essay in romance, but the achievement was in *The Scarlet Letter*, where the background was not splendid Rome but the arid, dusty Salem, Mass. And this, I suspect, is the reason why we are apt to be " put off " a little, if the first chapter of the new book has a Moated Grange or a Turreted Castle for its " scene," while we are drawn by an indication that the principal personages in the story live at Tooting Bec. And putting it higher still : he would be a bold author of these days who would write of man's first disobedience ; we, it appears, are to learn of high things, if at all, through little things, and things of low estate. If we are to see the vision of the Grail, however dimly, it must no longer be in some vaulted chamber in a high tower of Carbonnek, over dreadful rocks and the foam of a faery sea. For us, the odour of the rarest spiceries must be blown through the Venetian blinds in some grey, forgotten square of Islington; the flame that is redder than any rose must come shining on " Bolton Abbey in the Olden Time "—is that the name of the famous picture?—hanging over the mantelpiece in the Canonbury lodging-house. And be it remembered, I regard these old tales as true tales, true, very likely, in the very letter, and as true now as ever. But, speaking as a man who has dealt with some very difficult and delicate literary problems in his day, I would say that the more commonplace the setting, the easier the task. You are to make wonder credible; it is clear that if your setting, your scene, at least is credible and familiar and accepted you are so far forwarded in the work that is before you. At least we believe in Acton and know how to get there; but what is the number of the lines of 'buses that runs to Astolat? Book from Waterloo to Camelot? It is doubtful, I think, whether the tickets to Winchester are really available for the other place. The fact is, I suppose, that I am a determined realist, that I demand a certain degree of assent in the reader to the propositions which are laid before him. I am sure that if I had been a man about town in Grand Cairo somewhere in the twelfth century, I should have found the *Arabian Nights* the most credible book imaginable; credible, that is, in the artistic sense, as Micawber is credible, though there never was, in actuality, any such person. But I cannot read *Phantastes* with any relish, simply because it tells you in the first few sentences that there is not a word of truth in it; that it is an allegory and nothing more. Bunyan now, succeeds and arrests because he is so vivid that we forget all about the allegory even in the face of the allegorical tames of all the personages; the *Pilgrim's Progress*, is a masterpiece of the picaresque, of the wandering hero, who passes through frightful dangers and difficulties and comes to a very good end.

But again to the old notebook; as I ponder and delay over the Great Work on London. Again, I open it; I wonder at the infinite labours of former years; at the efforts renewed again and again which have issued in so little. Here, thick on every page, are the notes of stories which were never even begun. Thus:

MAZE STORY

Girl who danced in the Maze was afterwards beset by the influence she had in that manner invoked.

—after the Hawthorne manner, somewhat.

The maze was constructed on a wild, bare hilltop, with innumerable blocks of limestone. It was called " The Way (or Path) to the City."

And then a great bulk of notes and suggestions for " The Hill of Dreams."

He wondered whether all the objects of nature are not purely symbolical : whether nature does not endeavour to talk to us and tell us amazing secrets by the signs and cyphers of trees and ferns and herbs and flowers and hills and streams.

Suppose a Tuscan to come to a village of savages and talk in his beautiful speech, and suppose the inhabitants pronounced him a curious, gibbering creature and made him a slave to amuse the children by the strange sounds he uttered. Even so, perhaps, may be our state with regard to inanimate nature. The oak and the elm that we fell for our need may be wonderful signs : the brooks may indeed be books : the fern may be a great secret : the flower by the way the word of a great mystery : and whether we call the hills beautiful or dig coal from them, we may equally misunderstand their office.

THE LONDON ADVENTURE

And so on, pages on pages, long arguments, long lines of thought, heavy strivings to escape out of deep bogs and morasses, to get clear of false paths that led only to brakes of thorns; altogether the impression of a man who didn't know where he was going, losing his way in his endeavour to get there. Then: " The Hill of Dreams " at last finished, we begin again; we suggest plots for long stories or short stories on every page, thumping ourselves on the back all the time, and assuring ourselves that we can tackle successfully themes which would have appalled the very masters of romance. So here we go:

A " young lady " of a country town comes running headlong through a wood, in a state of wild shame and confusion at something she has seen.

She has been, contrary to her parents' wishes, to a certain spot disliked by the general opinion; there is a kind of superstitious dread against the place which has " hardened " into an instinct; people say it is not a " nice " place, without quite knowing why they disapprove of it.

It must have, no doubt, some relation to Roman times—to the fauns.

Some say it is " horrid "—" not a nice walk," Juniper bushes and Roman nettles.

Then :

. An " ethnological " story—would turn on the survival into our day of some primitive practice or desire.

For example :

An ordinary family living in the suburbs shut themselves up for certain days in the year to perform some horrible " cave " rites.

They have a language for these occasions, a " mystery " language : they have a code of morals, quite different from that of their everyday life.

They tear live animals for their food ; they write in " cuneiform " on tablets of clay.

They worship a concealed image which is locked up in a cupboard for the rest of the year.

Incident in such a tale.

Someone finds a broken piece of a clay tablet inscribed with the secret characters, on the road. It is shown to be modern, of clay found in the neighbourhood.

Who wrote the characters ?

You have heard the tempest of the theatre : have you ever seen the wind-machine : the silk stretched over a sort of barrel, which being turned round by the property man, shrieks and wails ? And here is another sketch for a terrible story :

Story of the man who made for himself a god ; building was going on in the neighbourhood ; foundations were being dug out ; and he begged a wheelbarrowful of clay, thinking he would like to try his hand at modelling.

He is rather an ordinary young fellow, but he has read, with a dim sort of interest, one or two curious books (so his mind is in a measure prepared).

He lodges in the suburb, has no particular employments, no absorbing interests.

His rooms are on the ground floor, opening on the garden.

It is one of those houses which stand in a garden with a wall all round.

He has a good many acquaintances, one an artist in whose studio he sees modelling being done.

He makes an idol : to pass " the time."

The story is : that he is gradually corrupted and destroyed by the idol he has made.

First his life gains a new flavour ; he becomes unconsciously an artist, and then, by degrees, an artist in sin.

He makes his idol foul, obscene ; feeling ashamed of himself as he does so, yet letting the whim guide him.

Here now, the notebook takes the form of a somewhat cruel parody.

(Clement Scott) (Gray's Inn Road on Bank Holiday night).

" He saw the street lit for a great solemnity: the music was wild as of a bacchic orgie.

" The whisky seemed an occult draught, thaumaturgic, tremendous, the wine of a mystery, changed from common drink and changing the initiate.

" He saw the shy girl come in, timid, happy, unwilling. . . . He saw her come out, her dress gaping, and a light in her eyes.

" And the music: it was only three barrel organs, a cornet at one pub. and a French horn at another.

" But it made an awful and appropriate harmony.

" There were howls as of wild beasts and shrill screams, the roar of a returning party in a brake, and hissing whispers in the crowd—this was the choir.

" It seemed that a rite was being performed.

" He came home and found an article awaiting him: it began:

" ' They were happy! Again and again they were happy! Who after this crowning mercy of a bright Whit-Monday will dare to repeat the calumny of the crusty chronicler ? Who that has seen our merry millions at play will venture on the time-worn jibe that the English take their pleasure sadly ? Possibly those superfine persons who bow down before the cult of the sunflower would have thought some of the fun a little rough, but who would give such persons a thought while there is fresh air on Hampstead Heath, brother, and sunshine at Greenwich ? ' "

And here is the outline of a nice Sunday-school story.

Story of the painter, who paints a picture, which he keeps hidden and concealed.

The lady to whom he is engaged comes one day to his studio by appointment : he is detained.

He rushes in, in a mad hurry, with an awful interrogation in his eyes.

She stretched out her arms and cried to him as he came in.

I think that is splendid ; and yet I cannot help remembering a criticism of a real author that a friend of mine once delivered.

" Yes," he said, " Edgar Allan Poe is wonderful, amazing; there has never been anyone like him. *But*, somehow, one is, now and then, inclined to laugh."

Now, for a puzzle: what is the mystery hidden beneath this " outline " ?

There was an old stone in the wood, on which she often found cottage-garden flowers scattered in summer-time.

She never saw anyone leaving the flowers.

There were cowslips and daffodils in spring; lilac blossoms, bachelor's buttons . . . in winter even, sprigs of box and laurel.

In summer great bunches of " old man " and cabbage roses and Sweet William.

Nobody in the village ever alluded to the stone or its offerings of flowers.

She was coming home late one night: heard a rustling, saw . . . a village girl (a singer in the choir) with a fresh posy in her hand.

She watched her lay down her flowers, and with staring, amazed eyes the ceremony that followed.

She found that nobody would acknowledge any acquaintance with the stone.

" The old people," she was told, " used to talk nonsense about it, a lot of silly superstition, I daresay."

She understood that there was a freemasonry among the frequenters of the stone.

And one day she went to the " houses " and cut curious orchids and many flowers of the steaming heat, and having made a wreath, went through the wood to the stone.

Here is the sketch of a little thing to be called "The Graven Image."

It was a burning hot day in Caermaen.

The river wound in and out, mystic between the reeds, in shimmering mist.

The blue-green woods were asleep and still.

The great mountain was in a dream. A deep silence, a hush of heat as if all the world were asleep.

Mr. X. and his friend Y. strolled out from the old house towards the walls, where the labourers were digging out a sunken tennis-court.

"We shall have a sloping bank all round to keep in the balls."

"Ah, what's that?"

It was a little bronze faun, preserved in almost perfect condition, in a layer of broken shards of pottery and dry sand.

Y. was enraptured. The find seemed fit for the day; it seemed to sing of the old summers when the vineyards glowed on the hill, and intoned the music of the flutes.

X. found it difficult to separate his friend from the statuette; he was willing to sit still, gazing at it, and finally he took it back with him, a present, to London.

It stood in a cabinet in his room. He vowed it had enchanted London, and that he could no longer see the dark fogs or the sooty air, but only the bright sunshine on the vines, and in place of the uncouth noises of the street, he heard Roman song.

There are many more of these shorthand sketches, and some of them were written, but most advanced no stage further. Then begin the notes for the book which afterwards became *Hieroglyphics*. The first sentence runs :

" Literature began with charms, incantations, spells, songs of mystery, chants of religious ecstasy, the Bacchic Chorus, the Rune, the Mass " :

and, to the best of my belief, the thesis of the book is fairly well summed up in the sentence. There are pages of these notes, " worrying out " the main idea of the essay with infinite elaboration ; and then things like this, which seem obscure enough :

He turned again to the monograph on *Labyrinths* : he looked at the plates : the various types of mazes (quote passage as to *dancing* with reference to mazes).

How does all this bear on the " psychology " : what reference to ecstasy : the drama : the lyric of incantation ?

THE LONDON ADVENTURE

It was a book that attracted him in spite of its dry, antiquarian air : he had felt that there was " something there."

Then the question of the *pattern*.

(Compare with the whorl, the spiral, Maori decoration.)

Why was this form common to all primitive art ?

The problem perplexed him. He took it, as was his custom, for a long walk ; and in the dreariest, most grey street of a grey, remote suburb, just as the men were coming home from the city, the thought, with a pang of joy, rushed into his mind, that the maze was not only the instrument, but the symbol of ecstasy : it was a pictured " inebriation," the sign of some age-old " process " that gave the secret bliss to men, that was symbolised also by dancing, by lyrics with their recurring burdens, and their repeated musical phrases : a maze, a dance, a song : three symbols pointing to one mystery.

Now, in the outline of this strange story—an ancestor, I fancy, of *The White People*—there seems some obscurity. As far as I can gather, the interest of the investigating sort of person, designated above under the somewhat vague style of " he," had first been attracted to this subject of labyrinths by seeing a girl, in the country—I am sure that the country in question was not far from Caerleon-on-Usk—drawing maze-patterns on the sand, or in a garden, or in her copybook. Now see what happens :

On D.'s—his name began with a D, then ?—reaching home after his long walk and his discovery, he finds a letter from Gregg (the country correspondent, I presume) telling him that the girl who had drawn mazes had disappeared.

" A hard-headed materialist, as you pretend to be, will no doubt be able to put me on the track. *Have you no suggestion to make?* "

The letter left D. in a swoon of amazement, and a beginning of shrinking alarm. After the theories ! He felt as a medium might feel who was suddenly aware that there was a real ghost in the room. He had called his theories credible, but was it possible that he would have to translate Latin into Saxon and confess that he *believed?*

He had determined that the maze was the symbol of a " process," and here, the girl who strangely seemed to know the meaning of the occult and antique sign had disappeared.

His mind went at once to the marvellous stories of magic transmutation, metamorphosis (Chants Scandinaves). He reflected how old the tales must be, of what secular antiquity, since human memory was so long. Persistently, the old stories told of those taken by *the fairies, rapt into the underworld*, recurred to him. He had rationalised all this into recollections

THE LONDON ADVENTURE

of the Turanian " little people," but their forts had been uninhabited for centuries. And the girl had disappeared ! What had happened to her ? . . .

The return : quite unconscious of what had happened.

" But it seems," said Gregg, " that the country people have superstitions about the place where the girl disappeared. There is some hill or other there that they call ——, and they have a tale of a woman who went there and never returned. . . . It is strange no one in the neighbourhood has come forward from first to last. She may have had money ; she may have come up to London ; she may have gone to Ireland. We really don't know."

And so the story that was to be *The White People* vanishes into dense obscurity, with bits of *A Fragment of Life* here and there embodied in it, in a strange and alarming manner.

And so I run through the old notebook, through dozens of these " hints " and " sketches " and " outlines " and " arguments," most of which led to nothing in particular. I find it all a little pathetic, and a little puzzling. I find my destiny a hard one. Here am I, born apparently with this itch of writing without the faculty of carrying the desire into execution. I am faintly reminded of one of Socrates' tremendous " scores." He had, in his usual bland manner, demanded a definition of happiness. A rash man comes forward and says, pretty easily and confidently, that happiness consists in the gratification of desire—and really, on the face of it, most of us would say that the definition is not much amiss. To want something badly, and then to get it ; to the natural man this seems happiness, or a very decent substitute for happiness. But not to Socrates. He pounced on the rash man, and said something to this effect :

" Then that beggar at the street corner must be happy above all other men. For he has the itch and vehemently desires to scratch himself, and he scratches himself all day long."

Whereupon the rash man—if memory serves—promptly collapses and gives it up.

But here am I much worse off than that Athenian beggar. I have the itch too, and vehemently desire to scratch myself, that is, to write, but I can't do it —save at long intervals, and after taking the most horrible pains, and racking my brains, and filling the fat notebook with hundreds of pages of plots and plans and elaborations and dark and crafty schemes. I dig deep, I burrow, far under the

THE LONDON ADVENTURE

ground, I hew out my laborious subterranean passages, I blast whole strata of unsuspected rocks which suddenly interpose themselves between me and my end, I dwell down in that stifling blackness of toil, month after month, year after year, scarcely emerging to see the light of the sun and the glow of the green world. At last, after all these dark and dreadful labours, I succeed in laying my mine. I touch the button—and there is a feeble pop, which would hardly make a kitten jump. And, pray let it be very clearly understood, that I do not mean by this that the published book did not make an enormous sensation and become a " best seller." I was never fool enough to look for that result. The kitten that did not jump was not the great reading public, but myself; it was I who realised that the explosion—the result of all these efforts was not, in fact, tremendous.

Long ago, at a tavern meeting—the good people will never credit what goes on sometimes in taverns—an old friend of mine said to me, over our beer:

" After all, we must agree that when God gives a faculty, He gives it with magnificent liberality. The measure is not stinted."

I think I agreed, to save the trouble of discussion, for it was past midnight—and " it is better to drink." But the dictum is not true, generally. Think of the immense number of the lives that have been poisoned and blighted by a stinted measure of faculty. I often ponder a saying of Oliver Wendell Holmes. He pointed out the misery brought about by a slight tinge of genius. " The man is spoilt," he said in effect, " just as fair water is spoilt and sickened by being poured into a glass in which there are dregs of wine." I would not limit the maxim to genius. The true tragedy is in the juxtaposition of desire and impotence. It must be horrible to long to write film scenarios—and to long in vain.

I repeat, it is all a little pathetic and a little puzzling. Most of us have always found the career of the *raté*, the artist who misses fire, distinctly comic. The poet who can hardly get into the corner column of his country paper, the novelist whose novels are simply " rot," the painter whose pictures are a joke ; we laugh heartily at them all. But, on the other hand, we are not in the least inclined to laugh at the small grocer who goes bankrupt, or at the widow with children who fails lamentably in the stationery shop—tobacco, sweets, newspapers, and fancy goods included—in the new suburb. I do not know why this is so.

The jests of the good God are sometimes obscure.

IV

IT will have been gathered, I think, from this book and from other books of my workshop that I am not altogether an enthusiast for the profession of journalism. Yet, looking back at those visions of strange places in London to which I have alluded, I am forced to confess that as a newspaper reporter I saw queer things and odd prospects which, otherwise, I should not have seen. In the general way, not in the direct course of the business, but rather as a side issue. Thus, I am sent to interview a distinguished fireman, who has just retired from the brigade with all honour—he had risked his life a dozen times or more, and had dreaded raging furnaces of flame as little as you and I dread the drawing-room fire. This is all very fine no doubt, and yet, by an astonishing paradox, the most tremendous heroism is a commonplace in man ; there are many men, hundreds, perhaps thousands of men, who are willing to risk dying the death of

THE LONDON ADVENTURE

the martyrs for two-ten a week—perhaps it is four pounds now—ready to face the roaring fires just in the way of business, as a bank clerk faces his daily accounts. This, astounding as it is, is commonplace, I take it; what was not commonplace to me was the infinite extent of Wandsworth. This fireman of whom I speak had retired from the Wandsworth Fire Brigade, and, fortified with his name, I approached headquarters in the old High Street of Wandsworth, in which I had lived thirty years before. The station gave me the address that I wanted, somewhere beyond the beyond of Wandsworth Common, and so I found myself traversing unknown and unconjectured regions, happy as always in the faculty of finding infinity round the corner of any street, within five minutes of anywhere.

I remember when I was quite a boy climbing up to a great mountain plateau in my country of Gwent. It was the beginning of the range that rises from the hollow of Pontypool and goes on swelling and falling and swelling to Abergavenny, and there dips down and surges up again and rises into sharp peaks of the order of the fairies and then marches onward in a solemn array past Llanthony, and so becomes the Black Mountains and goes into the very heart of Wales. But on this bright autumn day, just forty years ago, I climbed up into this high land—it was, in fact, a quest for a holy well still very famous in that country—I climbed up and up, and presently received that singular sense which always affects me in such places, the sense that all is moving not merely in space but in time. I mean, there comes a verge where the mountain visibly begins, where enclosures, hedges, fields, tilled and cultivated lands cease to be, where you come on the wild and know that you have come also into an older world before the time of sowing and reaping and gathering into barns. Up this big hill, then I went—it is only a big hill, really, though we call it down there, Mynydd Fawr, the great mountain—and came out from the fields of some hill farm, where they harvest, if they harvest at all, in October, into a queer lane. High banks, jagged limestone rocks and red earth on either side, oak trees, hideously dwarfed and contorted by winter winds; the bottom, huge slabs of limestone, with ravines between them where terrible December rains had torn the softer sandstone. This lane ended soon; and then the mountain began. Of short, sweet

THE LONDON ADVENTURE

turf, it surged up in a slow, steady slope, studded with dark green islands of gorse, glowing with their autumn bloom ; and then it still mounted towards another horizon ; and the dark green and rich gold of the gorse gave place to strange circles and patterns of grey limestone rocks, something dread, threatening, Druidical about them, though they also had their decoration of yellow lichens. And so onward, slope rising to a still higher slope and no end or limit that the eye could see, there in that high, desolate place, lifted far above men and their habitations and their tracks and fields and homely fires. And I remember—I was only twenty then— feeling that there was an expression for all this in words : " For ever and ever. Amen." It was not till very many years afterwards that I learnt that the Welsh for " and ever shall be " is " ac yn y wastad "—and into the waste, the waste of time being understood. And, it sounds farcical, but I could read something of all this text into a newspaper expedition to find a fireman in his little villa beyond Wimbledon Common. I do not think that I have ever consciously borrowed from Blake, of whom I know very little, I am sorry to say, but I do remember that he makes the Farthing Pie House—

it is now the Green Man, close to the Great Portland Street Station of the Underground—one of the limits of that Syon of his which is, somehow, London. But the unknown world is, in truth, about us everywhere, everywhere near to our feet; the thinnest veil separates us from it, the door in the wall of the next street communicates with it. There are certain parts of Clapton from which it is possible, on sunny days, to see the pleasant hills of Beulah, though topographical experts might possibly assure you that it was only Epping Forest. But men of science are always wrong.

And the mention of Clapton reminds me of a very strange and impressive scene I once witnessed there; this also in the course of my newspaper service. This, I should say, was not on those heights of which I have been speaking, whence one looks across a river valley to far wooded hills. This was in Lower Clapton, where it joins Hackney. My business took me to a great ugly hall, hideously grey without, painted within, if I remember, in dingy, bilious green, its gallery supported by cast-iron pillars. A raised platform or rostrum at one end, tiers of seats such as are in the gallery of a theatre behind it. In front of the rostrum something covered up with a blue and red flag; uniformed people grouped about this hidden object; above them massed bands with their bright brass instruments; the whole hall, floor and gallery, crowded; all the seats filled.

A Voice speaking from the platform :
" When I last saw her she was lying on her bed of agony in the hospital. Where is she now ? "

Another Voice from the hall :
" In Paradise."

Many Voices :
" Alleluya, Alleluya ! "

The first Voice again :
" The night before she died, they gave her clean, white sheets. She said, ' Oh, how kind of the doctor to send me these nice sheets ! ' I know who sent her those sheets. Who was it ? "

Another Voice :
" The Lord Jesus."

The first Voice :
" Because she was clothed in innocence; in the white linen which is the righteousness of the saints."

Many Voices :
" Alleluya, Alleluya ! "

THE LONDON ADVENTURE

The fact was that I was present at a great occasion. Major and Adjutant Jane Smith—I have forgotten her real name—had been " promoted to Glory." This was the funeral service at the Salvation Army Hall in Lower Clapton. It struck me as very remarkable, indeed; remarkable and impressive. Not so much because Jane Smith was, doubtless, a good and devoted woman, not because those who celebrated her faithful deeds and her pious end were, doubtless, good and devoted officers of the Salvation Army; but rather because of the form which the service assumed, that form being, as has been seen, a fervent dialogue. My mind was at once borne to another fervent dialogue :

Per omnia sæcula sæculorum.
Amen.
Dominus vobiscum.
Et cum spiritu tuo.
Sursum corda.
Habemus ad Dominum.
Gratias agamus Domino Deo nostro.
Dignum et justum est.

And here was the remarkable thing. You have at the one end the Jews and Greeks and Romans and the sweepings of all the Mediterranean shores that went to make up early Christendom; and at

THE LONDON ADVENTURE

the other end you have the sweepings of modern London, people, for the most part, of very indifferent education, people in poor circumstances, drawn from very grey streets and humble, circumscribed surroundings, by no means addicted to the study of the science of Liturgiology, people utterly unaffected by motives of the æsthetic kind, the last people in the world to like things " prettily done " —to quote the Tractarian lady in " Bleak House." And, above all, you have in the Salvation Army a set of people who have deliberately separated themselves from all ecclesiastical ways and customs and conventions, whose forms and phrases, so far as they exist, are borrowed from military terminology, who would regard a Methodist meeting as a rigid and cut-and-dried sort of business ; here are these people, quite unconsciously, reverting to Catholic ritual, to that fervent dialogue between priest and people which the logical and learned Protestants have always detested. I once heard a very different funeral service. It was Joseph Chamberlain's funeral, and the rite consisted of the Church of England service, with the Christianity omitted, delivered as a solo by Principal Jacks. It was all unspeakably dismal, depressing, deplorable, unmoving—because opposed to all natural human instincts. The Salvation Army has got away, unconsciously, from this strange Protestant perversion; it has become in this one respect at all events Catholic, that is natural, in the proper sense of the word. There is nothing more natural to man than " back chat "; and this remains true, even when the back chat is ecclesiastically termed " Versicles and Responses." The Puritan ministers of 1660 wanted to have the English Litany turned into one long prayer; they may have been very good people. So the folk who like to listen in silence to long-winded after-dinner speeches may be very good people; but the natural man wants to get a word in, to answer back, with an " Habemus ad Dominum," or some little thing of that kind. Of course, it may be said that, in the case of the speeches, the interjection of " Hear, hear ! " fulfils this need of humanity in an imperfect sort of way; and this reminds me of another service that I once attended. This was in a synagogue in the Commercial Road, down in the East End, and it was the Day of Atonement for the Sins of the People, and a very noble service it was. As I was rising to go, I had a whispered conversation with one of the wardens, concerning one or two points which were obscure to me, and I said finally :

"When the letters of the Name are made known there shall be Mercy and Compassion on every side."

To which he replied, cordially :

"Hear, hear!"

I think he must have been corrupted by our Western customs. I think he should have "responded" :

"For at His right hand there are pleasures for evermore "—or in words to that effect.

But I was saying, I think that the newspaper business, though, like the toad, ugly and venomous, has yet its precious jewels scattered here and there on its squalid vestments. And I remember one enquiry of mine causing me to feel quite dazed, bewildered, uncertain ; curious as to whether I had not somehow strayed into a world of illusion which was not wholly of our earth. For we, it is true, live in an illusory world, but there are other spheres of deception, beyond ours, and of a different order, into which we are scarcely meant to penetrate. So it is with the high geometry. I am sure that three-dimensional space is sheer fantasy and that a cube is as mad a dream as a griffin, or rather a much madder dream. But the geometers tell us that there is a fourth dimension beyond our three, and so on, as I understand, to the *nth* and to infinity; and I am sure that they are quite right—so long as we sleep, until we wake from nightmares to reality. But, in the meantime, I think that most of us prefer to take one set or order of illusions at a time, and are somewhat amazed and confounded at the intrusion of other systems of mania. I rather incline to think that the gentleman at the Mental Hospital who is, unfortunately, made of T.N.T. is a little disturbed by a visit from the other gentleman who is the Planet Neptune or, perhaps, the unrecognised Emperor of the United States of America. But: to our story.

In my newspaper days, I was on the reporters' staff of an evening paper, and the system or part of the system of such a concern is this. The gentleman who is called the News Editor—formerly the Chief Reporter—reads or causes to be read for him all the morning papers. Such items of news or comment that strike him as suggestive are cut out and pasted on slips. These are handed to the various reporters, and briefly, their business is to get something interesting out of the several matters that are handed to them. Thus, a brief paragraph may state that Trinity House has ordered that a Submarine Bell Buoy shall be placed off the Iron Reef, Morlach Head, where wrecks have been frequent. That much information strikes the morning paper as sufficient, but when I first became acquainted with evening journalism a dozen years ago or more, such an item of intelligence was one of the news editor's opportunities. A man would be sent to find out all about bell-buoying, to acquire accurate technical information, and then to make such information intelligible and interesting to the general public, as Mark Twain in his best book, *Life on the Mississippi*, succeeded in making the science of piloting a matter of high entertainment. This, then, was the older theory of evening journalism ; and so, one fine day I was handed a slip from a morning paper relating to some threatened litigation over a recent will. There appeared to be one or two odd circumstances in the dispute, and I was sent to " find out all about it," and " see the man," and " see these things which have been left him."

So, off I went, and, I think, took a ticket to Reigate, and in the train read my slip and pondered the case. Briefly: a Belgian gentleman named Campo Tosto—he was of Italian extraction presumably—had lived for some years at a house of moderate size some three or four miles from Reigate —if the town were Reigate. This house was in a hamlet called Burnt Green. Mr. Campo Tosto had been " looked after " by a man and his wife. Their name was Turk. Finally, Mr. Campo Tosto had made a will leaving all he had to Mr. Turk, and some relations had raised objections. I should mention that the Campo Tosto bequest chiefly consisted of objects of late mediæval art.

Very well; I hired a dogcart from a very pleasant old inn at Reigate and was driven to Burnt Green. Naturally—it was my business—I asked the driver if he knew anything about Campo Tosto deceased. Well, a little. " Rather a queer old gentleman; didn't like people coming about his grounds; would shoot at them sometimes."

" Shoot at them ! " I exclaimed. " Shoot at them with a gun ? "

" Well; now and then, with a gun; but mostly with a bow and arrows."

THE LONDON ADVENTURE

I made no more enquiries. Presently we came upon the fortunate legatee, Mr. Turk. He was evidently delighted with his good fortune. About him buzzed four press photographers. He was protesting vehemently. He wished for no more publicity. The press photographers declared that nothing was farther from their thoughts than press photography; and as they spoke, they took four shots of Mr. Turk. All this was on the King's Highway, just by the house where Mr. Campo Tosto had lived. I opened my mission to Mr. Turk. I found him still averse from more publicity, even of the written kind. He told me that he would tell me nothing, show me nothing.

"Except this," he added. "Give me that paper of yours." He took my copy of the *Daily News* out of my hand, deliberately turned it upside down—and read the article or the bit of news or whatever it was with the greatest ease and fluency. He explained his capacity of performing this feat—which, I may say, is a commonplace of the "Case Room" and the "Stone" in a newspaper office.

"You see," said Mr. Turk, "I was a farm-labourer for years, but lately I've had a lot to do with fuller's-earth."

But he would not yield farther. He allowed m
to walk with him up the drive of the house which
had been the residence of Campo Tosto, cunning
with the bow. I wheedled. The press photographers, cleverer than I, took more shots. Mrs. Turk
came out and denounced everybody. I was allowed
to look in through the half-glass hall-door; that was
all. Inside, I could see a huddle of fifteenth-century
Flemish Madonnas, brass altar candlesticks of the
" spike " pattern, carved oak chests. I drove back
to Reigate in a " dwam," as the Scots say; really
not knowing whether I stood on my head or my heels,
feeling rather like an actor who has been " rushed
on " for a small part in a mad drama which he has
had no time to study. For consider; here was a
man called Campo Tosto living in a place called
Burnt Green, which is, practically, a translation of
Campo Tosto. Here was a man whose property
consisted chiefly in Madonnas and mediæval candlesticks, who shot at intruders with the bow, either
long or short. Here was his heir, with the good old
English country name of Turk. And here was Turk,
who could read print upside down, because he had
been a farm-labourer and a worker in fuller's-earth.
I went home in that " dwam " and wondered what

THE LONDON ADVENTURE

on earth I was to do, and at last wrote the whole, true story, just as it happened, and ended by wondering whether it were, somehow, a parable, written for our example, though, as I said, I could not conceive what the moral of the story might be. But my news editor would not print it. As he said, gravely : " You must learn to recognise that sometimes there *is* no story. And, you know, you mustn't say that a man tried to read the paper upside down. That's virtually saying that he was drunk. That's a libel."

" But look here," I ventured. " This man didn't *try* to read the paper upside down. He read it upside down ; perfectly. You can't call that a sign of drunkenness : surely ? "

But the news editor shook his head. He understood, better than I, that one order of illusion must not be allowed to impinge on another. Anyhow, the singular tale of Campo Tosto and Burnt Green never adorned the columns of the Evening Paper.

Then, there was another odd adventure ; and this struck me as a difficult problem then, and remains difficult to me now, though I have no doubt there is a perfectly simple solution—if one happened to know it. This was the case of an inquest on the part of our lord the King. Not on a corpse; but on a certain Treasure-trove, found on the coast or seaboard of the county of Suffolk. I say, Treasure-trove, and to the best of my belief that was the matter of the Crowner's Quest, though I have often wondered whether it should not have been of Jetsam. But here was the case: there had been a great storm of wind and waters, and certain mariners hovering on the border of the sea had noticed bright objects shining on the sand, thrown up, apparently, by the great wash of the deep. They had leapt down from their place of observation and had gathered what they could between the waves, and it was found that they had secured a very interesting catch of coins. Here again was the cutting from the morning paper, and off I went to Liverpool Street, bound for the east coast.

There was no railway station anywhere near the desolate spot where this odd incident had happened. The station where I disembarked from the train was full six miles away from the shore, and, so far as I remember, the population it served was lodged in an inn and half a dozen cottages. I hired a man and a trap and drove off over a level country in bitter

THE LONDON ADVENTURE

February weather; the east wind blowing with the bite of the frost in it. It was fiercely cold, but I was a good deal warmed when the lad who drove me, talking of the crops of the country, spoke of " the peasen." Thank God! I said to myself, there is still some smack of old England left in the land. His father of a thousand years ago spoke of " peasen."

We came at last to a curious, desolate, unfinished-looking shore. Desolate? Hardly so dignified as that; there was no solemnity about its cold, barren raggedness. Sand-dunes, I think, but sorry sand-dunes, not big enough to be impressive; more a messy, sandy state of things than sand-dunes. There can be an awful solemnity about a region of sand-hills by a grey sea; but nothing of that here; it looked somewhat as if a speculative builder had heard that some people, with money, had got tired of wild, grey heights of cliff, and all that rather melodramatic, Wilson Barrett style of thing, and were going in for sand and coarse grass, and as if the said speculative builder had carried the sand to this stretch of coast at some expense and had sown the best kinds of coarse grasses, suitable to an eastern exposure. And, further, let us suppose that the speculative builder aforesaid had gone bankrupt in the middle of this enterprise, before he had got enough sand and grass together, and before he had run up more than three somewhat shabby bungalows. This was the aspect of that bleak and biting shore on the winter day on which I visited it, and lest I should be suspected of vilifying that Suffolk coast, I may say that Aldborough lay about five miles down southward, and that the shabby, starved poverty of that shore has been immortally set down in Crabbe.

The limit of land and sea is marked there by a cliff—if you may call it a cliff—rather, by a bank of sand ten, twelve, fifteen feet high. On this height, such as it was, the local fishermen had been standing a few days before, watching the raging storm and the great waves that blew in from the east. Suddenly, one billow, mightier than those before, had brought down a whole stretch of this sandy cliff. And as the wave washed back, the men on the inner heights noticed something bright and gleaming in the wash of waters. They retrieved what they could, and the learned being called in, pronounced that here were very ancient coins. I arrived, it seemed, in the very nick of time. I was shown to a chamber in a martello tower, and here were the men in blue jerseys and some sort of official personage, and they were counting out their find and sealing them into little packets—to be ready, I suppose, for the Crowner and his quest. And it was an astounding treasure. Far am I from being a numismatologist, but, to the best of my belief, the earliest coins in the find were dated of the eleventh and twelfth century. I remember noting a beautiful mediæval French coin, a disc of gold, with the lilies on it. But the dates went on in a sparse scattering way through the centuries ; here a coin, let us say of Richard I, then one of Henry III, then one of Edward II ; a gap perhaps to Henry VIII ; then a shilling of Elizabeth ; and so forth, and so forth. And then ; and here was the shock, here the true interest: two or three pennies of Edward VII, and a bronze medal commemorating the late Mr. Spurgeon, that esteemed Baptist pastor.

And, the questions are : what was this queer hoard ? How did it come to be gathered together ? Who gathered it ? How did the great wave discover it ? Was it washed up from the sea ? Or was it washed down from the cliff ?

I confess I find the problem almost as intolerable as the puzzles of Achilles and the Tortoise and the Lying Cretans. For, note, you cannot say that here was the collection of a numismatologist, even if you could get over the difficulty of such a collection being hidden in the sandy cliff or cast into the sea; both of them most unlikely places to keep coins in. For a man curious in old coins would never think of including the Edward VII pennies and the Spurgeon medal in his collection. To me there is only one tolerable solution, and even that is a very tentative one. The solution is this. A little way inland on that dreary coast there must be a well under a thorn or an elder tree. That well was once a Holy well, St. Somebody's Well. Those who made small pilgrimages to it and uttered their vows there were accustomed to drop offerings into the water. As time went on, the sanctity became hazy, the name of the patron saint was forgotten; but there was a lingering, decaying belief that there was something different here from the wells of common use. I remember a man of my age telling me that when he was a child, his nurse used to take him on an occasional walk to a well not far from Clifton. The small party would drink the water from their hollowed palms, and nurse would remark: "This water is so good that we ought to pay for it," and drop a penny or two into the well. And here, doubtless, was the odd end of a very old story. And

THE LONDON ADVENTURE

so, I conjecture—I do not know—that there was such a well not far from the Suffolk coast, that a wave drove in by a subterranean channel and, as it were, sucked the bottom out of it, and bore away, as it washed back to sea, the votive offerings that had been dropped there, even from the days of Cœur de Lion to the days of Edward VII and Mr. Spurgeon.

But the queerest story of all was connected only incidentally and accidentally with the affair of journalism. It happened that I was on some newspaper business when it fell out, but this was merely by the way. It was like this. My errand, whatever it was, caused me to walk from somewhere about Earl's Court Station up the Earl's Court Road—I think it is—to Kensington. To the best of my belief I had never walked that particular track before, during all the days of my life in London. It was in spring and keen weather, and I was wearing my heavy cloak. But the clouds parted and the sun shone out with a sudden heat, and I crossed over from the sunny side of the road to the shady. This action brought into my head Captain Morris's verses, which I quote from memory:

> Some may delight in the country to dwell,
> But give me the sweet, shady side of Pall Mall.

And that, in its turn, reminded me of a passage in Boswell.

"We walked in the evening in Greenwich Park. He asked me, I suppose, by way of trying my disposition, 'Is not this very fine?' Having no exquisite relish of the beauties of Nature, and being more delighted with the 'busy hum of men,' I answered, 'Yes, Sir; but not equal to Fleet Street.' Johnson: 'You are right, Sir.'

"I am aware that many of my readers may censure my want of taste. Let me, however, shelter myself under the authority of a very fashionable baronet in the brilliant world, who, on his attention being called to the fragrance of a May evening in the country, observed, 'This may be very well; but, for my part, I prefer the smell of a flambeau at the playhouse.'"

I was strolling along, thinking of this, and remembering that the fashionable baronet's title, given in a footnote, was Sir Michael Le Fleming, when I suddenly saw on a brass plate on the garden-gate of one of the houses the very name that had just entered my mind. Now it is very difficult to avoid lying in telling stories such as these. My impression is that the brass plate bore the inscription : " Mr. Edward—or John or Henry : not Michael—Le Fleming, Physician and Surgeon." But of this I am not sure : the name may have been " Mr. Edward Fleming," without the article. But, in any case, note the mad inconsequence of this odd incident. Here was I led by way of a heavy cloak and sudden warmth to the contrast between the sunny side and the shady side of the street, and so to Captain Morris's preferment of town over country, and so to a footnote in Boswell—and so to an uncommon name on a brass plate in the Earl's Court Road.

And, therefore ? Why, therefore : nothing at all. That is the interesting point, the highly significant point of the incident. I am reminded again of the incident of the Poltergeist in the Northern Suburb, since I have been reading only this morning an interview with the Bishop of Zanzibar, now, in this summer of 1923, in England. The Bishop, who talks all like a man, says there are queer things in his diocese. He speaks of strange wedding ceremonies in which the bridal procession walks over the mothers-in-law of the principals ; a curious matter, since I should have supposed that the ritual would have been reversed. But the Bishop had tales of things still queerer. He thought it might be easy enough to disbelieve in spiritual essences and powers exterior to man if one lived in England; in Zanzibar, he said, it was not so. He told a story, and I am sure that to the best of his knowledge, belief, and observation it was a true story, of a native mud-hut to which he was summoned. Briefly, the said mud-hut was disintegrating; not by the process of gradual decay, but in a manner of volcanic violence. It was flying into pieces, within and without, and nobody could see by what agency this was accomplished. Before the Bishop's eyes, as he went in, a portion of wall burst from its place and flung itself into the room. A piece of roof dashed itself on his head. Dr. Weston cleared the hut of all human inhabitants, and set a cordon of men about it outside, and still the place continued to " blow up " before his eyes. And then he fell to his exorcisms, and there was peace. And reading this; I remembered the broken kitchen window and the smashed crockery in the house in the northern London suburb; the frightened people, some wretched, some surly, who lived in that house. The Bishop did not say whether the mud-hut had a boy or girl amongst its inhabitants—it is likely

THE LONDON ADVENTURE

that this was so—but it does strike me very forcibly that if you are to be a Rationalist as to this Poltergeist business, you must commit yourself to a highly improbable hypothesis. For you are to observe that if these bangings and crashings and smashings are the work of conscious fraud a highly technical method must be employed, and a method applicable to very different circumstances and surroundings. There cannot be two places, I suppose, much more apart in all their scene and apparatus than the modest villa residence somewhere on the York Road line from King's Cross and the mud-hut of Zanzibar; and yet, the story in each case is, practically, the same story. It is possible, I do not deny for a moment that it is possible, that the London Poltergeist was naughty little Johnny, that the Zanzibar Poltergeist was naughty little Ngachuga; but how very strange it would be if it turned out that there was a secret art of smashing and crashing known to the budding youth of the whole world, and a very subtle art also, which enables the trick to be done under the very eyes of the annoyed and the deceived.

Now, Dr. Weston, of Zanzibar, was inclined by these circumstances to believe in the existence of spirits exterior to the human order, as distinguished from the ghosts of the departed. He said that some of the people in his diocese called them *Djinns*, and, oddly I think, thought it lucky to have one or two about the house, and were willing to pay good Zanzibar money to the medicine man to get such ghostly lodgers. As to this, I know nothing; but, if moved by the evidence of the northern villa and the African hut, we confess that there is something not quite explicable in this Poltergeist business; to what end do we come? Why, to nowhere. There is no *ergo* to the Poltergeist, there is no *ergo* to my strange, true tale of the Earl's Court Road. But I do think that in each there is a hint of certain things. We move, as I have said before, in a world of illusions, but of illusions on one plane. We are mistaken if we think that there is, in ultimate reality, any such thing as a cube, any such thing as a cow; but, at all events, these two are apparently on the same surface of being. But, now and then, there are intrusions upon us from other worlds, probably quite as illusory as our own. And we are accordingly left stupefied. There is no " therefore "; no *ratio*. Suppose a mathematician, in the high matters of his science, to come upon a conic section singing a comic song. Suppose a gamekeeper trapping weasels—and catching Abstract Triangles, or a classical scholar finding the optative mood turning into white mice, with small, gilt bells. Thus it was when the coals shot out of the coal-scuttle at Farringay on the King's Cross Line, when the mud walls broke upon the Bishop's holy head in Zanzibar ; when I saw the name " Le Fleming "—or Fleming— on the brass plate in the Earl's Court Road.

But, after all, from all this there does result this one moral, which may be regarded as more especially addressed to us writing persons—and our readers. And that is ; that the world, the sum of things of which we are cognisant, is infinitely queer, that even in the rind or surface of it the strangest essences are lurking, that tremendous beauties, amazing oddities are everywhere present, wearing very often, to use the Wardrobe Master's phrase, Disguise Cloaks of the most commonplace pattern.

To take an instance low down on the scale : if you take up a clever Detective Story and read how the hero or villain or the victim or somebody turns scarlet or green when the quiet little country curate comes up to him in the billiard-room, and says : " We're going to do the *Nunc Dimittis* in Stainer in A, after all " : if you read this sort of thing, I say, you are highly excited if you are a good man—I am an immense admirer of the early " Sherlock Holmes " myself—and you are on fire to pluck out the secret of the fantasy. But you regard it all as a mere fantasy; you don't for a moment believe that such things happen in what you call " real life " ; you are a little ashamed of being even lightly entertained by " such rubbish," you tell your friends how deeply interested you are in Gchkvof, and in psychoanalysis and in the new theory of poetical rhythms. But you are completely in the wrong. Such things are constantly happening in real life, or, at all events, in the only life of which we know anything. I have given a mild instance : after all, a curate may be expected to discuss the *Nunc Dimittis* and Stainer—unhappily, so far as the latter is concerned. But if I wanted to be severely " realist," I should make a shabby sloucher of the streets accost my man, ask for a fag, and then remark : " Why, then, guv'nor, if you haven't got a fag, would you mind telling me what Ateh Geburah veh Gedulah means ? " *That* is stark " realism," if you like. And the people who say that it isn't, really mean that they are more interested in vermin, skin disease, and incipient

THE LONDON ADVENTURE

dementia, which are the chief matters to be found in their favourite novelist Gchkvof. And, mind! I do not deny for a moment that these things are a part of the sum total of the world. I despise Gchkvof, not because he writes of lice and the itch; but because he does not understand the significance of either. These people, as Coventry Patmore said, dwell in surfaces, and they don't even understand their surfaces. If they were to make punch—they never would, preferring methylated—they would never comprehend what exquisite poetry of the palate may be obtained by manipulating a lump of sugar and the rind of the lemon and the orange.

And this instance is, as I have said, an instance low down on the scale. Ascend to the heights and think if that young, sick, under-educated apothecary and despised dabbler in verses, mooning one night in the suburban garden up at Hampstead. Think of the young lady close at hand, with her marked preference for the military as contrasted with the poetic character, sipping a little warm sherry and water with nutmeg before going to bed—and the chance bird singing in the shrubs of these raw villas. There you have the elements which issued as the " Ode to a Nightingale," by John Keats, to the great, though secret, terror and dismay of the people who maintain that Keats was silly—he was : that Miss Brawne was sensible—she was : and that nightingales can't help it—they can't. I beg pardon : these people cannot now say that Keats was silly, since he is a classic ; but they would have said so if they had known him in the days of his mortality. But it is curious, this reverence for the classic authors ; after they are dead. Two or three years ago there was a play produced that dealt with Shakespeare and other illustrious wits of the Elizabethan Age. There was a tavern quarrel, and some confusion in the business, as I suppose, made people think that Shakespeare was represented as stabbing another dramatist. They were horrified. And I have often wondered why they were horrified. Where is the incompatibility between writing wonderful, supreme poetry and getting into a rage ? And getting into a rage in the sixteenth century often meant drawing the little dagger. And why should not John Keats have been silly in his love affairs ? Even great and successful members of the Stock Exchange and the Bar and mighty leaders of industry have been known to choose amiss. It is possible to win the deserved title of " The Go-ahead Grocer," and yet have a secret taste for skittles or gin—and even for both.

Let us remember from this instance of the silly— or at least, mistaken—young apothecary poet, of the sensible young lady, of the whistling bird in the suburban villa, and, finally, of the well-known Ode, that the most amazing things are latent in the commonest, most everyday, ordinary circumstances; and, furthermore, that these amazing things are the only realities in the matter, and the only realities that do matter.

Strangeness which is the essence of beauty is the essence of truth, and the essence of the world. I have often felt that, when the ascent of a long hill brought me to the summit of an undiscovered height in London ; and I looked down on a new land.

V

I HAD just finished the preceding chapter, when I received from my learned and ingenious friend, Dr. Hubert J. Norman, a paper on " Genius and Insanity," a reprint, I believe, from the *Proceedings of the Royal Society of Medicine*. It begins with the statement that : " For many centuries it has been recognised that there is a definite correlation between genius and insanity." I wrote to Dr. Norman, thanking him very much, and denying everything, like Mr. Gregsbury in *Nicholas Nickleby*.

For, if we come to think of it, it is we, we others, the rest of us who are not men of genius, that should be certified and shut up. I was speaking of Keats, who made the Nightingale Ode out of his own somewhat misplaced passion, and his tuberculosis—if Dr. Norman pleases—and that commonplace Fanny Brawne, and the whistling bird in the grounds of the raw Hampstead villas ; well, that man, according to our doctor, is the madman, and we are sane.

THE LONDON ADVENTURE

Not so : if life be anything more than feeding and sleeping like a healthy and well-kept pig ; most utterly not so. And, frankly, if we adopt the extremest material view, we cannot say that human life, in its essence, is at all of the same order as the pigsty life. There are things common to both : pigs and men alike desire to be kept moderately warm in cold weather and moderately cool in hot weather ; to have enough wash or enough *consommé* ; and I am quite willing to allow that, ultimately, *consommé* and wash are the same thing. But there, if you think of it, the likeness stops sharp and finishes utterly. Let us be materialists if you please ; but if we survey mankind from China to Peru, according to Dr. Johnson's advice, we must admit that human existence mounts into scales and descends into scales that are altogether beyond the pig register. The Chinese, for example, may be very foolish in making beautiful porcelain, but they have done it for ages ; we must surely admit that making beautiful porcelain is human, proper to man, though not proper to piggery. And this vice—if it be a vice—of ornamentation is not the product of a late, corroded civilisation ; for all the savages that we know will put twirks and twirls and quillets on their domestic pots and pans; and the man behind the ages scratched the likeness—and a spirited likeness —of some prehistoric reindeer on a surface of bone; after he had gnawed the meat away. Really; it seems quite clear that Art, which, I take it, is equivalent with the genius of Dr. Norman's thesis, is in the very bones of humanity, that it is the *differentia* of man, that which makes him to be what he is, that distinguishes him from sheep and goats, that nourish a blind life within the brain. And how infinitely strange it is that we, who are men because we are artists, should begin to suspect that if we are artists we are mad. Genius, art are, I take it, vision; the power of seeing further, seeing deeper, seeing more than we others see, with the secondary part of expression, the power of communicating in notes, or paint, or marble, or words the thing that has been thus seen. What a very odd thing it would be if, now and then in a generation there were a man whose physical sight were telescopic, or microscopic, or both at once, who could read, let us say, the name on the ship's side while the vessel was three miles away, who could discern minute forms invisible to common eyes. And let it be farther granted that these reports of the keen-seeing man were amply con-

THE LONDON ADVENTURE

firmed by experience ; the boat comes into port and everybody can swear that her name is, indeed, *Phyllis Ramsgate* ; the microscope is applied to the object, and it is seen that the forms described are actually there. And then science steps bravely forward and assures us that the fellow is suffering from hallucinations. I think the analogy is fair : the creators of Falstaff and Don Quixote were mad —because they saw what we could not see in the heart of man, which we recognised as being infinitely and infallibly true, after the facts had been pointed out to us—by the madmen.

Ah ! If I had but been one of this happy race of lunatics ; how I would have shaken your hearts with the picture of Clarendon Road, Notting Hill Gate, somewhat bowery, somewhat stuccoey, vanishing into October mists and dimness forty years ago, on still, dull evenings ; with the picture of the poor lad who lived in the little top room of No. 23, issuing forth and pacing the dull, still ways, dreaming, ever dreaming and burning for the great adventure of literature ; seeing the stones glow into spagyric gold beneath his feet, seeing the plane trees in the back gardens droop down from fairyland, seeing a mystery behind every blind, and the infinite mystery in the grey-blue distance, where, as they tell me, for I have never sought to know, the street becomes dubious, if not desperate.

If I were only one of those elect madmen I should have known how to make that vague district that mounts upward to the east and the north from Gray's Inn Road as wonderful as that village of La Mancha, " the name of which I have no desire to recollect." I should have been able to give the sense and feelings of the lives that are lived there, remote from all the thoughts of London, from all its central and mastering aims and visions and ambitions. Here live, I know, the people who are a little aside from all our tracks, and, perhaps, some of them have a wisdom of their own or a folly of their own which differ from all our common systems of sapience or stultification. I remember a man of genius who, somehow, utterly missed his way, living in furnished rooms on the side of the steep, 1850 streets that ascend the hill, and he took me round to dingy rooms in Acton Street—where Andrew Lang records an undoubted ghost—and there I shook hands with a negro gentleman from the West Indies, who laboured under a very strong suspicion of leprosy. Apart from this unfortunate black man, who, I hope, was wrongly suspected, I always look upon this strange, unknown region as the country of the people who have lost their way. For example : supposing you are meant by nature to be a tremendous Wesleyan, the Wesleyan who gets into the papers, and stands in the forefront, who is interviewed constantly and is heard at the Central Hall where the old, wicked Westminster Aquarium used to be, who meets Anglican bishops on terms of equality ; and supposing that the moving finger writes that, after all, such is not to be your fortune : then you live in a dim square in the quarter I have indicated and attend the services of the chapel of the Countess of Huntingdon's Connexion, situate close at hand. And here I see Blaydes, who was doing quite well in the City in 1890, earning his £200 a year, with a promising love affair with a girl employed in the Daisy Insurance Company—she was one of the earliest of women to take to a clerkly life—I see Blaydes watching poor Gladys as she died of consumption in her chair, babbling, as she died, poor soul, of the hat she meant to buy for Easter ; I see Blaydes, who had found a very nice villa at Sutton, with very creditable neighbours, certain to call, who dreamed of the children that were to be, and the social amenities and the sense of stability, the sense of having stayed the dreadful clock of eternity, so long as one clung to that good, red, square villa in Sutton, Surrey, of having stayed that awful clock for a little while, at all events, while one clung to Sutton, Surrey : I can imagine that hapless Blaydes drifting to two rooms in one of the steep streets—I think in the house that has a fine Chinese junk in ivory in the ground-floor window—and living on there for forty, fifty years ; a broken, bemused man, who answers most politely when you speak to him, and then says nothing, and dies away into grey silence and the grey region receives him and holds him for all his days.

I am sure that they are all secret people who live there, to the east of the Gray's Inn Road ; secret and severed people who have fallen out of the great noisy march of the high road for one reason or another, and so dwell apart in these misty streets and squares of 1850, wondering when it will be 1851.

And then there are places and regions farther afield, places on the verge of London, as unknown to the vast majority of Londoners as Harran in

THE LONDON ADVENTURE

Abyssinia. To attain these, the general recipe is to take something that goes out of London by the Seven Sisters Road, something that touches on Finsbury Park, which, I take it, is the extremest mark of the *Londinia cognita Londiniensibus* ; the caravanserai from which the caravans set out across the wilderness ; the merchants telling tales of travellers who journeyed on just such a voyage and travail and were heard and seen no more of men ; though some chroniclers, in the fashion of old Mandeville, and therefore not to be trusted overmuch, hardily affirm that these very rapt personages have been noted going to chapel on Sundays in Grinders Green, wearing silk hats and frock coats, or as doing their own marketing on Saturday nights, haggardly, awfully, as men dwelling under the command of a *djinneh*, on the heights of Tottenham Rye. Such tales they tell of them that scoffed at the predictions of the geomancers, and undertook the journey of the great caravan that sets out from Finsbury Park, a station on the Great Northern Railway—I have not duly noted its new name—from York Road. His Name is the Merciful, the Compassionate, the King of the Day of Judgment ; and in the Halls of Eblis there is no backyard gloomier than the backyard in which York Road Station, King's Cross, is situate. O true believers : be not misguided by those who speak proudly of Euston and Somers Town : for they stray from the way of truth.

Alas ! I am sane, as the doctors persist, and so I cannot show these visions.

But, in sober truth, this equation of madness with genius seems to me in itself a very violent form of craziness. For, if one examines the facts and takes the great names : Shakespeare, Cervantes, Milton, Fielding, Molière, Dickens, Thackeray, Keats, Wordsworth, Tennyson : what an evident lie it all is. I am quite ready to allow that men of great power of mind have gone mad, that many second-rate poets have gone mad ; but many first-rate farmers have gone mad, many agricultural labourers and plumbers have developed symptoms of dementia. The fact is, I suspect, that we others, who have no genius, have an instinctive horror and dislike and a kind of dim, unrecognised envy of those who have it. If I were an undistinguished major, not over smart with my men, I think I should be soothed by the scientific assurance that Julius Cæsar and Napoleon were, after all, only high-class lunatics.

THE LONDON ADVENTURE

It is I, the major, who am the perfect soldier, the normal soldier. It is true, indeed, that there is this common bond between some—not all—men of genius and madmen. Each fails to see the objects of earth under his feet, the one because his eyes are dazzled with light, the other because he is stricken blind.

But here we are, still delaying over the great work, *The London Adventure*; and nothing done. I begin to reflect on the matter very seriously, as the summer wears on. It strikes me that I had better try an old recipe of mine, and start out, on a book of a totally different kind, in the hope, I suppose, that the one undertaking, going prosperously—as of course it will—may stimulate the other. I search my mind; I go back to an old notion on which I set my heart far away in the 'nineties of the last century. This was the symbolising of a story of the soul by the picture of exterior things. I would write of a man on his summer holiday, if you please, granting him of special grace a month instead of the usual fortnight. I would write of him as coming to my old territory, and as he ran down the shore of the Severn and the level lands to Newport noting something strange, in the shape of the wild Grey Hills to the north, something outland in those greeny dells of Wentwood, that hide in their lower slopes buried walls and temples. I would take my man to Caerleon-on-Usk and show him the grey Roman walls mouldering there above the green turf, and show him the red sunset over the mountain, and the tawny river swimming to the flood. He should go wandering away, this unfortunate fellow, into such a country as he had never dreamed of; he should lose himself in intricacies of deep lanes descending from wooded heights to hidden and solitary valleys, where the clear water of the winding brook sounds under the alder trees.. He should be high on Mynydd Maen in the morning, in the fullness of the sun, and drink in the wind that blows there, and look out on the rolling billows of the land, and far down yellow Severn Sea; and finally he should come home again to London and perceive that wonderful things have been wrought in him; that these woods and hollows, these ancient walls and buried temples, this might and majesty of sun and wind upon the summit of the great mountain wall, these enclosed, still valleys of hidden peace and wonder; that all these things have discoursed to him a

THE LONDON ADVENTURE

great mystery, whereby his soul has been renewed within him.

That is a tale that I have been thinking of telling since the eighteen-nineties, as I have said. It is only now that I have finally realised that I shall never tell it. Dear Cinara's dear reign is ended.

But then there was another notion, a very queer one. I have said in another place how much amazed I was when I realised in 1899-1900 that my books were coming home to me in an odd way enough. Casual acquaintance, hitherto of the most ordinary type, meeting me in the purlieus of Gray's Inn, would utter terrifying sentences which would remind me of *The Great God Pan* at its worst. Publishers earnestly requested me to found secret societies; Miss Lally and the Young Man in Spectacles became my constant companions, uttering astounding things and involving themselves in the strangest adventures; I found, with something of a shock, that I was living more in *The Three Impostors* than in Verulam Buildings, Gray's Inn.

Well, I was thinking the other day of these queer doings, when I remembered another circumstance, equally odd, as it appears to me. In 1896 I was deeply engaged in trying to write *The Hill of*

Dreams. It was in the June of that year, and I had plunged into the difficulties of the "Roman Chapter," where the hero—or idiot—of the story is rapt into the ancient Roman world of Caerleon, and listens to the music of those corrupted flutes, and walks on marble pavements that have been for so long broken underground, and drinks from such rich, curious cups as Caerleon churchyard now ostends—when they dig old Owen Morgan's grave. My man had seen the city walls, now grey and ghostly in their æonian decay, all firm and white and shining, and had heard the pealing of the trumpets when the watch was set, he had been a part of the ringing tumult of the tavern by the river, where the priests of Osiris muttered their secret jargon to one another. Very well, indeed ; or as well as could be expected in the circumstances. But, remembering all this, there came into my mind a queer affair. I was deep in all these matters, as I said, in that June of 1896 ; and after one very heavy and terrific night at this dismal old game of invention, I went out for my customary midday stroll in the Gray's Inn—Bloomsbury quarter, still struggling in my mind with my Roman problems, and whimsically considering—without the smallest real belief, I may say—a vague shadow

THE LONDON ADVENTURE

of an intimation I had received the night before that I was really present at the Latin play in the hollow theatre by the river ; I was musing over all this, when I suddenly became aware that I had utterly lost the sense of direction. I was disoriented, though I was in a part of London most familiar to me ; north and south, east and west had no more any meaning. I knew perfectly well that I lived at 4 Verulam Buildings, Gray's Inn ; but as to where Gray's Inn was, considered from the view-point of—say—Lamb's Conduit Street, I had not the remotest notion. I got home somehow by complicated and dubious calculations, and in a somewhat confused and alarmed frame of mind. And odd as it may seem, this perplexity has never wholly left me. I emerge from the Tube Station at Oxford Circus, and take my bearings from All Souls', Langham Place, and thence, by a kind of dead reckoning, find my north or south, east or west.

So, here was the notion. What about a tale of a man who " lost his way " ; who became so entangled in some maze of imagination and speculation that the common, material ways of the world became of no significance to him ? A fine notion, I think : but dear Cinara's dear reign is over.

THE LONDON ADVENTURE

So here ends, without beginning, *The London Adventure*; and, indeed, I have been in London all this summer of 1923. I had thought of calling the book " The Curate's Egg," but I have a distaste for boastful titles.

Printed in Great Britain at
The Mayflower Press, Plymouth. William Brendon & Son, Ltd.

Works by
Arthur Machen

❖ ❖
❖

The Hill of Dreams, 7s. 6d.
The Secret Glory, 7s. 6d.
Far-Off Things, 7s. 6d.
Things Near and Far, 7s. 6d.
Hieroglyphics, 7s. 6d.
The Caerleon Edition of the Works, £9 9s.

Martin Secker

Works by
D. H. Lawrence

The Lost Girl, 9s.
Women in Love, 9s.
Aaron's Rod, 7s. 6d.
The Ladybird, 7s. 6d.
Kangaroo, 7s. 6d.
England, My England, 7s. 6d.
New Poems, 5s.
Birds, Beasts and Flowers,
  10s. 6d.
Sea and Sardinia, 21s.
Psychoanalysis and the Unconscious, 5s.
Fantasia of the Unconscious,
  10s. 6d.
Studies in Classic American
  Literature, 10s. 6d.

Martin Secker

Date Due

PR6025 .A245L6
Machen, Arthur
The London adventure

263910